Errant in Iberia

Journeys through a new life in Spain

By Ben Curtis

Errant in Iberia

For Marina

Errant in Iberia

Author's Note

This book was written when I had been in Spain for three years, and is based on impressions gathered in notes and journals from those early days. Please forgive the occasional anglicisation of names, and the odd accent missing from Spanish words.

B.C.

Life Before Madrid

It started at New Year, the same year I eventually arrived in Madrid. I was living in London and determined to spend the annual anti-climax abroad. Equipped with a cross-channel ferry ticket for my car, with a trip to Germany in mind, I very nearly went in entirely the wrong direction. But then my German girlfriend and I parted company at the last minute, in the desperate setting of Waterloo station, and everything changed.

She was waiting for me outside a newsagents near the Eurostar terminal, and as neither of us had the enthusiasm to do anything much at all, we ducked into a filthy-carpeted basement pub off the station's central concourse. I sensed doom, felt terribly lonely, and within no time at all we had talked our way out of a nine month relationship.

She said, 'You're too much of a dreamer these days, always in the clouds. I've had enough.'

'I know,' I replied, and couldn't really think of any convincing reasons to carry on with the whole thing anyway. Inwardly I blamed London, but compared to excuses like another woman, boredom, or a change in sexual persuasions, I didn't think that a capital city would seem very convincing.

In a fortnight we'd been due to head off for New Year on her parents' farm, where I hoped to meet the cow she had ridden around on as a little girl. There had been that to look forward to, but it was obvious that neither of us could even face a holiday together anymore.

So it had finally fizzled out, in the most unpleasant place to split up with someone ever known to man: a dank, beer-stained pub, full of shabby Essex businessmen who had deliberately missed another train home to squeeze in an extra pint before facing family life at home.

I saw her onto a double-decker bus under the station arches, was briefly gripped by a panicky urge to jump on after her and try to unravel all the wrongs, but walked away instead, through a light London drizzle, feeling thoroughly depressed. Something had to change.

With Germany ruled out, the ferry tickets led my friend Tom and I on a long drive to Spain, crossing the border from Andorra, high in the Pyrenees, on 31st of December, 1997. Nothing much at first. Just cloud cover, thick fog and isolated villages whose defining feature was rain. Then we picked out a tiny road on the map, the C1311, that would lead us in the right direction. Immediately the monotonous Pyrenean gloom cleared to reveal a precarious road perched on the edge of an infinite vista of arid, broken foothills that stretched scraggily into the distance - it looked like an image of the American Badlands. We passed a flock of thin, floppy-eared sheep, then spotted our first Spaniard, a shepherd, an ancient man squatting by the side of the road who raised an arm and smiled. I was smiling too, caught in the clutches of a fairy-tale landscape, entranced.

We drove all day, down from the mountains, over endless empty plains, past contours and colours I had never seen before, chiselled gorges shifting to endless horizons, fields of swirling purple and red earth - so un-Northern European, what happened when you crossed the Pyrenees? - and finally, in darkness, we arrived in San Sebastian.

San Sebastian, sitting on the Basque coast in the crook of the right-angle formed by the change from Atlantic France to Spain, invites dreams about the world before civilisation came and stamped out its eternal mark. I imagine what it would have been like to be the first men to descend on the place, when there was nothing but woodland and sea. To have stood on the city's central headland and gazed left across the wide horse-shoe bay with its little conical island, and right, to the long stretch of sandy beach on the other side. To have looked out over that interminable sea, shifting with fish and erupting with the odd passing whale (all fished away long ago by the industrious Basques). Behind, only a tropical carpet of forest would have rolled up to a ring of distant mountains that cut off the rest of the world, if indeed there was any world beyond this. There needn't have been. That view is almost the same today, if you ignore the city that, albeit elegantly, spreads back from the beaches.

There were three of us now: Sheila had been living there for almost a year, sculpting, teaching, and surfing. It being New Year's Eve, and us being English, we started celebrating rather early, sitting in her damp flat tucked high up behind Gros beach, drinking wine and poring over her plans for a larger-than-life-size man, to be shaped in resin, marble or glass.

At half past eleven we raced down to the beach, popping into a petrol station on the way to pick up a couple of bottles of Cava - the Champagne from Spain - and to marvel at the wisdom putting a beer-vending machine in a place almost exclusively frequented by drivers.

Where were all the people? It was nearly midnight, there wasn't a soul on the streets, the bars were shut or empty, and not a single party could be heard anywhere. A group of teenagers fired rockets at us from the top of a beach-side apartment block, but then they ran out of fireworks and disappeared as well. We went down onto the sand and huddled beneath the concrete alcove of a summer beach bar, while the Atlantic battered away at the shore in front.

It was possible that we were the only ones on the streets in the whole city. Sheila explained that all the good Spaniards were at home with the family, heading for the climax of the year's biggest meal. At twelve we opened our Cava amidst something approaching a gale. This, I decided, was already the best New Year's Eve I had ever had. Far better to be bearing the brunt of a storm on a Spanish beach than suffering another dreadful end of year party at home. Then at last the locals came out to join us, and things improved even further.

In half an hour the city changed completely. Just about where the British start winding down, overcome by alcohol, exhaustion, and Auld Langs Syne, this lot began to get going. As we wandered into the old-town's maze of blustery streets, endless fresh young faces streamed past. Constant chitter-chatter, the throwing of heart-stopping bangers, a buzz of beautiful features; everything was propelled by an energy I had never known before, that picked you up and carried your spirits along at shoulder height. I love this place, I thought, as we drifted from bar to bar.

The whirlwind continued all night, until seven o'clock in the morning, when I found myself being sick into a gutter. I had taken to my new surroundings with a little too much gusto, whilst the locals, as bright-eyed as ever, showed no sign of slowing. We did the big walk around the town's three bays that afternoon, strolling above La Concha beach in twenty degree sunlight, as I reflected very unkindly upon life in London.

Brixton Blues

When we got back to England two days later, stepping out of the car into Brixton's Mackie Road, I felt a despair that cannot ever risk being repeated. The sun, wherever it was, had been turned right down, at the mercy of some divine dimmer switch. All was grey, damp, January, and dour. I had no job and no idea what to do about it. The days melted again. Everyone going out to work except me, the gate snapping shut as they left in the morning, Mark's cough receding up the road, then Tom's, then silence.

For the past three years I'd been trying to survive as a professional photographer in London, trying to turn a life-long passion into a job. Unfortunately, it seemed that photographic talent had very little to do with earning a decent living. Much more important were hard-nosed business skills, like tireless self-promotion, and a fiercely competitive streak. Still, I managed to pick up the odd bit of company portraiture, which paid silly sums for very little work, and came along once every couple of months.

Like all young photographers in London my dream was to see my work in one of the Sunday supplements, or on the cover of the latest super-band's hot new album. (Actually we all wanted to be like David Hemmings in his "Blow Up" role, driving around in a Rolls Royce and snapping away at rapacious models that were desperate to sleep with you after the shoot). I dragged my portfolio round to the big newspapers and several record company art departments, gathering polite refusals, "it's great stuff, we'll let you know..." They didn't, and I gave up. Had I returned time and again, doggedly harassing these people with sparkling new images, then who knows...

On one heart-stopping occasion I came home to find a message on my answer-phone from one of the biggest music labels.

Message: "Hi Ben, we're just putting together a new cover for our latest act, we think it's going to be a pretty important release, and we remembered those great sepia images of hands and trees that you showed us. We'd be really interested in using one of them for the CD."

I was over the moon until I realised that I didn't have any sepia images of anything at all, and indeed, a quick phone call revealed that they had phoned the wrong Ben. A few weeks later I arrived home to find Tom in a mood of over-excitement.

"Ben, check out the message on the machine, I can't believe it, you're totally sorted from now on!"

Message: "Hi, Benjamin, this is John from Virgin, we're putting together the art for a pretty important project, I'm not sure if you were aware that the remaining Beatles were reforming and that we've signed them for the first major release. Well, we think you're doing the kind of work we're after, so please give me a buzz on……"

"Can you bloody believe it?!" said Tom.

"No," I replied, "that voice belongs to Simon from college, he was having a laugh."

"Oh."

To keep myself busy amidst all these brushes with success I signed up with a film-extra agency, and soon got my first roll. I was a foot-soldier in another King Arthur TV movie. Having spent two hours playing dead in a freezing puddle on a mock-up battle field in Pinewood Studios, I was sent home early for laughing too much in the middle of a pitched battle. I was laughing out of pure nervousness, as my sword-fighting partner was going at it tooth and nail with his all-too-real looking fake weapon, and I thought he was about to take one of my fingers off.

"CUT!" screamed the assistant director, "You think this is fucking funny do you? Do you think you would have been laughing in real life, in King Arthur's time? Go on, bugger off my set, idiot…"

My first taste of the generosity shown towards the lower castes in the mighty hierarchy of the film world, where the extra is nobody, another prop to be shunted on and off set when required and shouted down at any available opportunity.

Still, the next film, Shakespeare in Love, proved to be the highlight of my short, two-film career. With the long straggly hair I was sporting at the time the casting department had no doubt in pin-pointing my 16th century persona: a Wharf Dog, being one who hangs about doing nothing on river wharfs. So, dressed in rags, I spent several weeks lounging around in a big tent with hundreds of other scruffy lower class Elizabethans, waiting to be called on to perform our duties as background figures in the mock-up of ancient London, or as unruly figures in a theatre crowd. Like all extras we spent the day protesting, that we were only there for the money of course, that this was just a side-line while our *real* jobs had temporarily cooled off.

There were painters, musicians, writers and even the odd aspiring actor, all hanging around for hours on end, desperate for lunch to be called 10 minutes late so we could pick up another bonus payment. There is a scene in the film when hundreds of peasants are walking towards the theatre, and I alone am walking in the other direction – fame! When I saw the film with friends at the cinema, however, I was the only one not to spot myself.

When I wasn't busy 'working' I would spend time mooching around in the gloomy house I shared with two friends at the top of Brixton Hill. Off they would go in the mornings to their proper jobs, something I swore vehemently I would never get, whilst I eventually rolled out of bed, sighed at the grey London skies, and resigned myself to a long, hot bath. What remained of the mornings would be spent dreaming up great new plans to acquire better photography assignments, and hoping that the film-extra company would phone me with another day's work, anything to get me out of the house. Then I would wile away the afternoons rearranging photos, again, for my next killer portfolio, the one that would lead to a job with National Geographic, that kind of thing.

Or maybe I'd go for a bicycle ride. A nice trip down to central London, passing those signs on the way: '*Appeal for witnesses* - Arson committed at 192 Stockwell Road... Shooting on Tulse Hill...' and my all-time favourite, 'Man grievously assaulted and thrown into the Thames...' By the time the others returned I'd usually fallen into a combined state of complete boredom and personal crisis, soon quelled with a bottle of cheap red wine.

For some time this hotchpotch of general non-activity had marked the general rhythm of life in London. It was dispiriting to say the least. As soon as Tom and I got back from Spain, I fell back into the same old routine. A few months slipped by without me noticing. I was a background dot in a couple of TV series. All I could think about was the nicer country I had discovered on the other side of the Pyrenees.

Then two things happened that finally put the boot into life in the British capital, the first involving a girl, and the second photography.

The two last straws

In a previous incarnation as someone who had just got out of university, who was presented with a small amount of money from his Grandparent's will, and had no desire whatsoever to get down to anything much in particular, I had buggered of to Thailand to learn how to dive. Life on a desert island was far preferable to making a start in London, as all of my less fortunate but (in retrospect) far wiser friends were doing. So off I went with another trustafarian colleague and found myself on a rather nice little coconut-fringed island in the Gulf of Thailand. Nothing to do all day but look at beautiful fish, gorge ourselves on Thai food, and wile away the evenings drinking beer and smoking the local tobacco. It was paradise, and completely undeserved, though I like to think now that this lazy decadent lifestyle was accounted for later, by three years of confusion in London.

Still, at the time I was happy to ignore the future and continue my climb up the diving-world ladder. Within a couple of months we had paid our way through enough courses to become "Dive Masters". What's more, we were quite happily ensconced on our island by now, knowing quite a few of the locals and most of the other western drop-outs. We were even paid small sums for helping out in the dive shop. This was the professional life for us, not like those mugs in the UK, and what's more we were picking up valuable skills, like how to eat raw Thai chillies and cloves of garlic whilst swigging away at Mekong, the fiery local whisky.

Then, just as things seemed like they couldn't get any better, along came Katie - young (four years younger than me), blond, gorgeous, and usually to be found in a pink draw-string bikini. By way of providence, or divine generosity, Katie and I got drunk one night and she ended up spending the night in my bungalow. By the end of the week she had moved in, and there she stayed, another glorious indulgence, Katie and her quick-release bikini, until we all left the country two months later, penniless and even a little tired of paradise.

Back in the U.K. I made an obvious, easy and erroneous decision: to move up to London where all my old friends, and Katie, were now living. As with all good problem-page holiday romances,

Katie and I didn't last a month in our new surroundings. No sooner had I done the rounds of my friends with my tanned, blond bombshell, than she informed me that she had found someone much more interesting to hang around with, an older man she'd met in a club who was fond of driving her around in his Porsche. That was that, London depression number one. I should have taken the hint and left there and then.

Three years, a few photography courses, lots of unemployment, a German girlfriend, and a New Year trip to the Iberian peninsular later, I was lying on the sofa one afternoon dreaming of my escape to Spain when the phone rang.

"Hello"

"Ben? Hi, it's Katie!"

"Katie! My God, how are you, how did you find me?"

"Your mum gave me your new number, I'm in town for a few days, back from Uni, and I was just wondering if you fancied a drink tonight…"

"Ah… alright, definitely."

It wasn't long after arranging to meet down the road from my house that my mind wandered back to tropical nights and quick-release bikinis. I began to wonder if her home in West London wasn't just a bit too far to get back to once the tube had closed - perhaps she might need a bed for the night. Things had been rather quiet since my German girl and I had parted company, and at this stage even ex-ex-girlfriends were an exciting prospect, regardless of whether they had dumped me, depressed me, and phoned up three years later as if nothing had ever happened.

And so we met up in the Cat Bar (not it's real name, but close), a central Brixton cool-person hang out, where vodka and tonic flowed all night into chunky crystal glasses. It was one of those places that I was really beginning to hate, full of unspeakably pretentious white rich kids with cool weekend drug habits and first mortgages, who weren't to be confused with normal people in provincial towns with weekend drug habits and first mortgages, because this lot lived in *Brixton*, which was 'predominately black', and 'cutting edge' and dangerous.

Katie returned from the bar with two vodka and tonics (ice and a slice), and we started, predictably, to relive those Thailand memories, a clean version of course, not the triple-X late-night bungalow-antics version that had been replaying in my head ever since her phone call. And of course she looked fantastic in her short, tight dress, and was definitely flirting a bit, unless I had got things really wrong… By our fourth v/t, as the underground closing hour drew near, I was starting to feel quite hopeful. Katie went to the lavatory, and came back grinning.

'Alright?' I asked.

'Yeah… Sort of… Something really odd just happened…'

'What?'

'Well, you see that black guy over there in the denim jacket?'

'Yes.'

'He just followed me into the toilet and offered me a go on his crack pipe.'

'He *what*? What did you say?'

'Yes, obviously. We went into the cubicle and he gave me a quick blast. I'm feeling a bit out of my tree at the moment!' She grinned, ecstatically.

'Jesus,' was all I could think of saying. Living in 'cutting edge' Brixton and being used to bars like this I wasn't at all surprised or upset by people doing drugs, but crack was one of the big no-nos, a taboo, it was one of the really 'bad' ones, that only screwed-up people played around with. It meant yardies, gun-crime, and crack-babies. And here was Katie, my ex-ex- and possible fling for the night, willingly doing the stuff in a toilet cubicle with an extremely dodgy-looking, complete stranger. I excused myself, in shock, and also went to the toilet, making quite sure I wasn't followed by frightening men with evil plans to corrupt me.

When I got back Katie's cubicle friend was sitting in my place, while she sat, wide eyed, listening to him. Seeing me, he got up and left.

'Alright? He wants to know if we're after any coke, says he'll give you a free line if you want,' she said.

'Um, I think I'm probably alright thanks.' Coke was just a step down from crack in my books, though widely used amongst the first-mortgagers.

'Go on, don't be so boring. Anyway, I think he kind of thinks we owe him after my freebie just now.'

'Oh God. Look, I don't like coke, I'm happily drunk, and we definitely don't owe that bloke anything!'

'Suit yourself,' and off she went again to the toilet.

Oh what had happened to my lovely night with Katie! To innocent memories re-lived over a few quiet drinks with an old girlfriend, followed by a chance night of passion? Clearly Katie was to blame for starters, a couple of years in a fashionable south-coast university had taken its toll. But there was more to it than that. London was at the bottom of all this. Only here in this devilish city could very hard drugs and dubious characters crop up so easily and screw things up. I was angry with her for getting so wasted when she had come out to spend time with me, but I was far angrier with the Cat Bar, with Brixton, with London life and its dirtiest habits.

'Ooh dear,' she was back again, 'he came into the cubicle again, gave me a couple of lines for free, I think I can safely say that I'm wasted!' And she looked it: happy, bug-eyed, on another planet. And now he would definitely think we were in his debt, and let's face it, what with this being Brixton he was almost certainly armed, properly armed that is, 'tooled up'... I was starting to feel extremely nervous. 'So, do you want anything off him then?'

'No, let's get out of here.'

Out in the street, she put an arm round my shoulder as we walked towards the main road.

'I think I must have missed the last tube,' she said.

Now was the moment, when I was meant to say, 'your welcome to stay up the road with me if you want, I'll give you a lift back in the morning...', but instead I hailed her a taxi. I just wanted to get away, from her and from every aspect of crack-infested Brixton and its seedy take on normal life. I thought she looked disappointed, though it's hard to tell with someone that's taken so many happiness-inducing chemicals. Still, I was sure that my night of passion would definitely have been on the cards if London hadn't come along and mixed my sex life up with hardcore, class-A drug dealers.

That was the first of the last straws.

The photographic incident occurred shortly afterwards. One day there was a knock on the door, and I got my last photographic job, the one that changed everything. It was Jon, our lanky, middle-aged, South London neighbour .

'Alright Ben. What you doing with yourself this week?'

'You know, the usual.'

'Oh yeah, busy then?'

'We're going to take that rubbish out of the back garden, if that's what...' It was a recurrent worry for Dave's wife that our back garden was lowering the tone of the neighbourhood, and in summer we were constantly reminded to mow the tiny patch of lawn.

'No, no, just wondering if you were working much, that's all.'

He thought I too was a drug dealer, that must be what this was all about. Seeing me at home day after day, driving a half-decent car, it couldn't possibly make any sense to them otherwise.

'What about tomorrow for example? Day off?'

'Um, it's looking that way at the moment.'

'Only, we want you take a few pictures of the family. We'd pay you of course.'

'Great! what did you have in mind?' Thank God, I was innocent after all, and what's more, here was a job!

'We thought we'd offer you fifty quid for a few nice portraits of the family.'

Disappointing, but thinking quickly I calculated that if I got all the pictures on one film, then gave them the prints and negatives to sort out their own enlargements with, then I'd make at least forty pounds profit!

'But we want decent prints, off one of your professional laboratories, no one-hour rubbish.'

Profits dropped to twenty quid, but still, I couldn't refuse.

'O.K. Right. Tell everyone to wear colourful clothes, nothing too dark or too light, terrible for photographs,' I said, as he retreated down our front path.

The following evening, the first thing I noticed as I trooped into Jon's teak cabinet, M.F.I. living room was that his wife, Carol, was wearing an off-white blouse and his dumpy, twenty-something daughter was dressed head to toe in black. Both looked like they had just returned from a particularly flamboyant perm at the hair dressers. Overnight I had remembered that taking tacky family portraits was, professionally speaking, scraping the bottom of the barrel, and the scene that now presented itself gave me an intense desire to bolt for the door.

The dumpy daughter was trying desperately to cheer up her two children, twin boys of about five, Carol and Jon's grandchildren. They had been dressed up in bright green shirt and red bow ties, which was probably why they were crying. The dog, a medium sized poodle with weeping red eyes, was having a yellow ribbon tied round its neck by Carol.

'Doesn't my boy look lovely Ben?' she said, referring to the dog.

I started by taking a series of simple portraits, black-clad daughter on navy blue sofa against dark green and gold curtains. That was going to come out well. Then Dave and Carol, a few of the 'lovely boy', and finally, when they had been sufficiently quietened down with promises of jaffa-cake biscuits, the five-year-olds.

'Right,' said Carol, 'now the really important one, all of us together. Make this a good one, Ben, we're going to blow it up and frame it for the wall.'

Carol and Jon stood proudly behind the sofa, whilst the dumpy daughter and the five year olds sat in front, surrounding the poodle. '*Jaffa cakes*', hissed Carol to ensure her grandsons' continuing collaboration, '*jaffa jaffa jaffas*'.

'Quick,' said Jon, 'while they're laughing!' I lined up the camera, reached for the button, and froze. Right in the middle, centre frame, my eye had been caught by an object of such extreme unpleasantness that I could barely bring myself to look back through the viewfinder. The poodle, perhaps over excited by having his picture taken, or even by the mention of all those jaffa cakes, was nonchalantly displaying the most pink, pencil-like male-dog erection that I had ever seen. There it was, and only I, and the camera, could see it.

'*Come on!*' said Carol, from behind a clenched smile. We all knew that at any moment the grandsons' good humour would fail for good, but this was a picture that I could not possible take. I pretended to adjust a tripod leg, looked up again and nothing had changed. I winced and mumbled something about film speed, whilst thinking desperately how to tell them that the dog was not at its most photogenic. They couldn't understand for a second why I wasn't taking the picture, and all but the two boys began to stare at me murderously, until suddenly, just as Dave was about to start swearing, one twin swiped at the other, who punched back at the first, and both children burst into tears.

That was it. Carol threw her arms in the air, Dave rolled and re-rolled his eyes in demented circles, and the fat daughter screamed at the boys as she fought to tear them apart. Still the dog sat centre stage, serenely calm and terribly excited as all hell broke loose around him. How I regretted later not pressing the shutter release at that exact moment.

There was only one thing to be done after that, forget the photographic profession, ditch London, and get off to Spain as quickly as possible. It was a place where I imagined I would go and spend a long time abroad, where I might take innumerable photographs *just for fun*. It was a place where people didn't throw each other into freezing rivers, where bars didn't have carpets and where, in January, the sun came out.

Paris - Madrid

Not long afterwards I found myself at Austerlitz station in Paris. London was a safe distance behind me (but not yet far enough), Madrid some fourteen hours ahead. Soon the *Francisco de Goya* night train would whisk me south through France, spirit me over the border at Hendaye whilst I slept, and finally, soon after I had woken up, deposit me slap-bang in the middle of vast, unknown Spain.

I was sitting in the station buffet, eating a limp goat's cheese salad and sipping *vin rouge*. Waiters buzzed amongst piles of suitcases, taking orders from animated French families and screwing up their faces at foreigners. It felt like the last supper. I was already loosing my nerve. I knew France, and French, yet despite that wonderful New Year in San Sebastian I knew less than a dozen words of Spanish and couldn't imagine a life in Spain. Beautiful, romantic Paris... It gave everything to everyone. If I just stayed here, wonderful things would surely start happening, most involving parties with writers, and delectable French girls who would say all the right things at exactly the right moments in *that* accent. I mean, I only had to get the bill and I could disappear into those chic Parisian streets forever.

Earlier that afternoon I had spent three anxious hours on the Eurostar, wondering just what on earth I was really doing as Kent, the tunnel, and finally Northern France slipped past the window. A busker on the Metro from Paris Nord to Austerlitz momentarily restored all faith in my journey, when he belted out three rounds of *Viva España* on a battered Clarinet (*'We're off to sunny sunny Spain...'*). This bode extremely well, and I gave him a big tip. But now I was getting worried again. What possible need was there for me to go to Spain? Oh God, I thought, did I really have to go that far away?

I boarded the train. The French girls would obviously have to wait. Anyway, I had an important mission in hand, to seek out the train manager and acquire a once-in-a-lifetime treat, an upgrade from tourist class to a single, private compartment. A good night's sleep would be more than worth the increase in fare. Who knows how I would arrive if I had to share a standard four-berth compartment with anyone from rampant molesters to serial psychopaths?

The carriage guard showed me to my new, first class accommodation, then did his best to bring me straight back down to earth.

'What are you? American?' he asked, as he folded down my bed. I told him I was English. 'It's all the same,' he said, 'too much money.'

Paris disappeared quickly once the train got underway, replaced by muffled suburbs and empty countryside. I sat on the end of my narrow bunk, looking out of the window and trying to catch typically French images in the fading light - symmetrical rows of tall trees, concrete telegraph poles and fields of maize. At ten I wandered down to the dining car, a comfortable, rattling carriage decked out in cream plastic panelling, blue nylon curtains and fold-away cinema chairs. I sat opposite an old, glamorous looking French lady who was buried in a crossword, and didn't promise much excitement. Then two dream-like figures appeared at one end of the carriage, tall African gentlemen dressed in gold-embroidered brown robes and pink cotton bobble hats. The waiter directed them to the two empty seats at our table.

They spoke to each other for some time in a dialect or patois, until the older of the two suddenly turned to me and, in perfect English, asked where I came from.

'England,' I replied, 'and you?'

'Nigeria. This is my son, I am showing him around Europe, it is a great experience for him. We have been to Paris and London so far. It is a holiday and an adventure. Also we are hoping to buy shares in convenience food companies.'

'Yes,' said the son, 'I already own one enterprise at home, and now I would like to expand over here.' (How old was he for goodness sake? Maybe nineteen?) 'Do they eat much bread in Spain?' His face was calm and composed, his English slow and measured, like his father's.

'Well, yes, I think they eat quite a lot actually,' I said, trying to sound sure of my facts.

'Good, that's good news. Bread is a very profitable convenience commodity. Where might I find suitable companies in which I can invest?'

'Well. Perhaps your embassy could help you out... or maybe there's a Spanish/Nigerian Chamber of Commerce.' I felt pretty pleased with that, but they didn't look at all convinced.

'Anywhere else?' asked the father.

'Ahh... the Yellow Pages?'

'Yes. That's what they told us in Paris.' We gave up on the business chat after that.

A hundred kilometres and one invitation to Nigeria down the line, my bill arrived. Theirs didn't. The train manager had taken care of it. What noble princes, I wondered, were these? With exactly which share-hunting, bread-and-biscuit empire builders had I had the honour of sharing a table? I went back to my compartment, and resumed my place at the window.

Curious fellow passengers, Agatha Christie-style, the unseen outside world slipping past in a shroud, occasionally casting up a dim cardboard skyline, a spray of lights, with luck the odd name of a station taken at a slow pass, these are the thrills of the night train. They all combine to create whatever landscape the imagination desires, while other travellers fall perfectly into their role as whatever rogues, runaways, romantics and Kings that you feel you ought to be travelling with.

Arriving early the next morning after a restless night locked up on my own, I ran into the Nigerians on the platform. Gone were the robes, replaced by designer track-suits and trainers. Had they slept well?

'Oh, no,' said the father, 'my boy spent the whole night staring out of the window.'

The son was just an ordinary nineteen-year-old again, with a wondrous look in his eyes. I said goodbye, walked a little way up the platform, and stopped. I was suddenly terrified. I knew no-one in Madrid. They were princes on a business trip with untold wealth at their disposal and here was I with nothing but a vague plan, something along the lines of 'go to Spain, take photos, see what happens.' It was 1st September 1998, my birthday.

≈

Later, around midnight, I was sitting outside a cafe in a small oblong plaza, drinking a last, unnecessary whiskey and soda. It was an extremely warm, still night, and couples wandered past on their way to the Plaza de Oriente gardens. A blonde, female security guard was pacing up and down in front of me, by a side entrance to the solid, granite expanse of the Opera House. Every now and again a musician would hurry out of the glass swing doors, clutching an instrument case in their hands. I was just watching a young, lady violinist rush off into the night when the first Dane sat down opposite me. He was grey haired, plump, and obviously drunk.

'Have you got some problems?' he said.

'What...?'

'Never mind. We are trade unionists, from Denmark.'

His friends pulled up chairs, closing in all round, one fatter and chuckling, one tall, moustachioed and German sounding, distinctly camp. Another, the oldest, carried a pouch that contained six pipes which he rotated continuously in a feat of constant smoking.

'And you, where do you come from?' continued the first.

'England.'

'English! Ha! Do you know the Iron Lady?' Once they had run through all their Thatcher jokes, and given up on trying to buy me another drink, it was to the pipe-smoker that all the attention turned.

'I am getting married next week,' he announced, 'and have never made love to a black woman!' At this they collapsed into a drunken, leg-slapping hysteria, whilst I, exhausted, decided to make my escape.

Since getting off the train that morning I had spent the day walking the streets. I made a twenty minute visit to the Prado museum. By the time I had located Goya's black paintings I was so overwhelmed by tourists and the sheer size of the place that I left. Instead, I went to the Retiro Park and scuffed up the dust on the dry paths near the lake, resting occasionally beneath a tree, to keep out of the exhausting afternoon heat. I wondered if I would ever speak to anyone ever again. I decided that Madrid was too hot, far, far too noisy, and that under no circumstances should one be fooled by the oh-so-strikingly good looking girls, because sooner or later, as in all Mediterranean countries, they would surely change cataclysmically into their mothers.

Then late in the evening I had found the terrace cafe in the square beside the Opera House, and set about celebrating my birthday beneath a Martian September sky. The clouds were so low, or perhaps the city so high, that the two appeared to be seamlessly joined, producing a marshmallow, kaleidoscopic roof, lit bright rusty red by city lights and loose energy from all the frenetic activity below.

Now, walking towards my hostel, up a cracked cobbled street lined with tall, decaying old apartment buildings, I was troubled by the

Dane's first question, 'Have you got some problems?' No, I reminded myself, I had no problems at all. I had spent an important day alone in a strange city, but that was fine. The Danes had just caught me in a contemplative state, wondering what to do with myself. An American tourist had once found me like this in London, thinking, whilst peering down at the waters of the Thames from Battersea bridge. She quickly engaged me in banal conversation about the view, where I was going, where I was from, anything, until I finally made an excuse and left. It was only afterwards that I realised in horror that she had actually thought I was about to hurl myself into the River! I had just been staring blankly down, considering my options, nothing else. My contemplative look obviously needs some work.

It was really pure chance that I had wound up in Madrid at all. Once I'd decided to change London for Spain, I realised that I would have to earn a living, and that without a word of Spanish, English teaching was the only possibility. But I would need to be taught how to teach. I made enquiries about doing the 'T.E.F.L.' (now 'C.E.L.T.A.') course abroad, received a prompt reply from an academy in Madrid, and was told I could start in three weeks. Now that I was here, on the eve of the start of the course, I had decided on four options for what lay ahead, and it was these that I had been contemplating when the Danes arrived.

Option one: to complete the month's course, enjoy the hard work and make the most of Madrid, then to leave, having never used the qualification to teach a soul. Two: to do the course, then travel around Spain taking marvellous photos on the way, and finally to go home via Paris. Three: to finish the course, get on a train to the coast, and get a job (this being the preferred option). Four: to leave at once, literally flee, before the course even started, head straight back to Paris, get a job, and marry a French girl with *that* accent (this was the most intensely desired yet wholly unrealistic option). Not for one minute did I consider that I might actually stay in Madrid. This, I believe, is quite common.

'Still thinking strongly in terms of Paris', reads a scrap of paper that I scrawled upon that night when I got back to my hostel, and below that, 'Going to bed to dream of the slim lost ethereal red haired girl with the rucksack that I saw after breakfast.'

A Room Over The Plaza Mayor

I soon discovered that a good way to end a night out in Madrid was to wander down to the Chocolateria San Gines, a regal, marble and mirrors cafeteria tucked away in an alley off the Calle Mayor, where they served hot battery Churros sticks and thick, blamanchy hot chocolate. This worked wonders on an impending hangover and besides, was a Madrileño tradition and not a bad place to get one more emergency drink at six o'clock in the morning.

But better still was to head up to the Plaza Mayor afterwards. By this time it would be entirely empty, peaceful, and glowing with the same hue as that autumnal Martian sky. Then, without the tourists, the plagues of *terraza* tables, the drunks or the buskers, it required little imagination to see it as it was, in various incarnations from the past.

Above the cobbles of this broad, majestic square, below the four storeys that enclose it on each side and the curious murals on the northern facade, the Inquisition had burnt thousands of their prey. Once, neat gardens had sculpted out a little urban park. In another era trams trundled through one of the mighty granite horseshoe arches, crossed the Plaza at a fair tilt, and rumbled out again, down towards the Puerta del Sol. Looking around I could almost hear their echo, almost smell the box hedge that once marked out my path, and looking down at the grime, I would imagine the martyrs' ashes, trodden hard into the ground over the centuries.

This was where Eduardo told me that he really lived. He worked in the hostel where I was staying, and seemed to spend most of his life in a little room that was deemed too small for guests. It was next to my room which was only marginally larger, musty, as hot as an oven, and devoid of a single stroke of imaginative decoration.

His room, however, was carefully decked out with a single bed, hand-printed Indian covers, bookcase, telephone, Persian carpet, and the continuous smell of joss. In here Eduardo would spend his evenings, supine on the bed, book in hand, a lotus eater content with the minimal demands of his job. He had an intellectual, Roman profile, a thin beard and greying hair combed hard down to his neck. His

English was near perfect, and he supplemented his income with a handy sideline in unofficial breakfasts.

Whenever I came through the hostel's front door he would appear suddenly and ask me about my day. By the middle of the first week he had discovered that I was learning to teach, and on the basis of the fact that he too had taught Spanish for a decade, moved me sympathetically into the biggest room in the hostel. Now I had tall windows and balconies onto the street, a large table at which I could work, and, the *piece de resistance* - en suite bathroom aside - a Michelangelo-esque angelic fresco painted onto the ceiling above the bed. There I lay for several nights, congratulating myself on this earthly paradise, thinking that it would do nicely for my month in Madrid.

Eduardo began to take me into his confidence.

'Hello! Hey, you should see the two Hungarian girls that took a room today, Wow! And you know what, they took a room with only one double bed!'

The other employee was a young man called Rafael, an athletic bloke who was often seen wandering around with a pot of paint. To Eduardo, he was a constant source of both irritation and respect.

'Hello, how are you? Listen,' said Eduardo the next day, 'you won't *believe* this, you remember the Hungarians?'

'Yes.'

'With the *double bed*?'

'Yes....'

'Rafael, that bastard, he... you know, he... yes! *both* of them, at the same time!' He wrung his hands and disappeared back into his room.

As well as keeping me up to date on Rafael's antics, the benevolent Eduardo continued to consider my accommodation. He did his sums, and worked out that he could certainly do better than the hostel prices.

The following day he appeared as usual.

'How's the room?'

'Wonderful,' I said.

'Really? Good, I'm pleased... good. And you're here for a month?'

'Yes.'

'I told you that I lived on the Plaza Mayor, didn't I?

'Yes, I think so.'

He leaned over the desk and lowered his voice.

'I may have a better place for you. I live up there in a big flat with an extra room, right over the Plaza,' he paused a moment and looked over his shoulder, as if someone were listening. 'It's a nice room, I sometimes rent it to students from the same school where you're studying. I was going down there this week to put up an advert, but thought you might be interested first. Cheaper than this place you know.'

I didn't know what to say. I was pretty settled with the fresco room, in fact I wasn't sure that it could be bettered.

'Come and have a look if you like, I'll show you it, whenever you like. How about this evening?'

A room over the Plaza Mayor. At least it had to be worth seeing. He told me the name of a small bar in a quiet street nearby.

'Meet me there at seven,' he said, and stood back to attention behind the desk. 'By the way,' he added, 'that Rafael, my God, last night he was in bed with a Japanese girl, the one in room 2! *Ay* what a bastard.'

I never saw any of Rafael's alleged conquests. The hostel occupied the first floor of an old apartment building near the Calle Mayor and the only other guest I ever saw coming in or out of the other rooms was an aging clown. He went out every evening dressed in full costume, carrying a bucket of roses under one arm. These he sold to tourists in the bars and plazas of the old town. He had lived in the hostel for as long as anyone could remember.

The whole business with Eduardo's flat involved a highly covert operation, as he was, after all, trying to poach three weeks custom from the hostel. We met at seven in the specified bar. He whispered to me in steady English, as if in code, that he would charge me slightly less than the hostel, that the room was the best in the flat, and overlooked the Plaza. I tried to hide my growing interest. With suitably serious tones I swore that I wouldn't breath a word to Rafael (who was starting to get to me too), and told him that I thought that I had better have a look.

We entered via a low, heavy wooden door on the Cava de San Miguel and climbed a winding, seventeenth century granite staircase. As we passed the first and second floors, peering through the arrow-loop windows, I wondered if I should have told anyone where I was going. Absolutely no-one knew where I was. Another heavy door led into his third-floor flat. What if he was some sort of weirdo? He marched me straight to a large room at the end of the hall corridor, threw open the interior shutters with a flurry, and opened the balcony doors. There at our feet lay the Plaza Mayor, buzzing with all the circus-business of a warm September evening. Waiters ministered briskly to the tables below, tourists puzzled over maps or embraced, in one corner someone was breathing fire, in another they played guitar. From one of the towers came a curious peel of bells, drifting easily across the soft murmur of a thousand voices crisscrossing the plaza below.

'This,' he said, 'is the room I have to rent.'

'It's nice,' I said, 'when can I move in?'

≈

The teaching course was going remarkably well. I was learning a lot about concept check questions, integrated skills and the information gap, but at least my brain was stretched for the first time in years, and now I had people to talk to. There were twelve of us altogether, including three American girls, a Scot, a Canadian, and, strangely, two Spanish girls, who probably spoke more accurate English than any of us. In the morning we were lectured on grammar and methodology, in the afternoon we were tortured. It was called T.P., teaching practice, and involved real-life, proper teaching.

On the second day I found myself standing up in a classroom and speaking to a group of real people, something I had studiously avoided throughout my entire life. It was somewhat akin to an out-of-body experience. There was I, or what seemed to be 'I' at least, in front of the white-board trying to hold the attention of a mixed bag of teenaged and adult students, while my tutor and fellow trainees sat at the back actually taking detailed notes on my very first performance. Meanwhile, the real me, the spirit of me-ness, felt like it was cowering in the corner, eyes tight shut, quite unable to accept what was going on.

Still, everything appeared to be going O.K. We were playing some sort of get-to-know-each-other game. I was giving instructions and they were doing exactly what I said. Incredible. Then Nacho, the grinning young man from Peru, put up his hand.

'Excuse me?'

'Yes?'

'How long have you been teaching?' Everyone stopped what they were doing. I - both 'I's in fact - froze on the spot. He had seen through my thinly veiled act to the fraud beneath, it was all over!

'A... About 7 minutes,' I said, and the whole room, students, tutor and trainees, burst out laughing. Somehow, it became a lot easier after that.

I would walk back to Eduardo's flat in a daze, shattered after the day's mental bombardment. My route took me past the porn shops of Chueca, across the raging traffic on Gran Via, and down past the haughty disinterest of the prostitutes on Calle Montera. Being Britishly unaccustomed to such matters, I was particularly surprised by the prostitutes. They may have been for the most part overweight and ugly, but that wasn't the point. The fact was that they just stood around on one of the city centre's busiest shopping streets, ignored by everyone but the odd lamentable client, who would be led off to a room in one of the squalid side streets. This was all part of the fascination for Madrid that I felt on those walks home. There was a real crackle to the place, an electric charge, something like the extravagant and volatile atmosphere of New York, that has you pricking up your ears and widening your eyes, eager to round the next corner and to know what lies at the bottom of every street.

But still my original four options weighed heavily upon me. With my month's training racing along, it would soon be decision time. Under no circumstances did I want to go back to London, but I worried that I lacked the courage to seek out a job and stay. How was I just going to roll up in some beach town and procure a job? At least the return to Paris, and the French wife that accompanied it, had long since slipped my mind. Spain it was, or bust.

Back at the flat I would usually find a note from Eduardo. 'Try this wine, and put on the C.D., track 10.' Thus in his prolonged absences at the hostel he introduced me to the essential accompaniments to a bohemian life above Madrid's Plaza Mayor: Eric Satie, Monteverdi, a glass of his favourite Rioja. On the occasions on which our paths crossed he would talk about the book he was reading, who Rafael was sleeping with, that sort of thing. Sometimes he would tell me dark tales from Mexico, where he had studied the potent effects of the country's most hallucinogenic mushrooms. He had even written a thesis on the subject.

At regular intervals throughout these conversations he would become incensed by a busker who had taken up at one of the cafes below. He would whirl round and step out onto the balcony in a rage.

'You bastards! Hey! You! You try living here and listening to your shit all day, you imbeciles!' Then he would run to the kitchen for an egg that, to my horror, he would land with startling accuracy on the unhappy guitarist's lapel.

'Live here long enough and these people drive you *craaaaazy*!' he roared, marching over to the phone. He would call the police, have it out with them, then calmly resume our conversation, returning every now and again to the window like a dog making sure they had seen off an intruder. Usually, however, after a further exchange of crude gesticulations, the offending musician played on unperturbed.

At the end of September I sat outside the Opera House, at the bar where I had spent much of my first evening in the city. A lot had changed. There was a chill wind in the air and it felt like everything that was everything a month ago had been swept away on the rising breeze. The academy where I had spent a month learning how to teach had called me aside on the last day of the course and offered me a job. It was another covert operation. I wasn't to tell any of the other trainees. I accepted without reservation, and signed a nine-month contract on the spot. All options removed from the equation, just like that. In retrospect it was either a miracle, or just another example of how easy it is to end up stuck in Madrid. Probably both.

How Many Bars?

Living in Madrid it's easy to gather facts, statistics. Madrid is the highest capital in Europe (627m above the sea level at Alicante), and Spain is the second most mountainous country on the continent, after Switzerland. This is, of course, the noisiest city in Europe, and there are more Basque surnames in the Madrid telephone directory than there are in San Sebastian's, that emblematic Basque seaside stronghold. But the one set of statistics that it is hardest to pin down, that varies so wildly in comparison to the rest, is that which concerns the number of bars in Madrid.

There are over nineteen thousand bars in Madrid, someone will tell you, while I have heard another put the figure somewhere nearer a quarter of a million, which obviously seems absurd. There are more bars in Madrid than in the whole of Belgium, which fits nicely with 'There are more bars in Spain than the rest of Europe put together'. Which, if any, of these is true is utterly uncertain. What is clear though is that there are a phenomenal number of bars in Madrid, and that the city wouldn't be itself without them.

They are the hearts that pump the lifeblood through the city, and at breakfast, mid-morning coffee, lunch, tea, and suppertime, they set Madrid's pulse racing. On Friday and Saturday night, so frenzied is the activity in any one of these who-knows-how-many establishments, that to the new arrival, the city, and every one of its four million inhabitants, seems to be on the point of cardiac arrest.

The archetypal, all-purpose, identi-kit Madrileño bar, is equally at home in the city's poshest quarter as it is in the slummiest, and just as popular in both. It has none of the living-room feeling of the English pub, but an easy-going functionality based around a long zinc or wooden bar-top. The more zinc, the plainer the bar. Behind the bar hang entire legs of ham, trotters and all. On shelves beside them sit an impressive range of spirits, to be poured freely and in dizzying quantities into tall straight glasses. One make of beer, and one only, will be available on tap. On the work surface, in a glass display case, sit trays of tapas - octopus, anaemic looking sausages, cod stewed in tomato, potato salad - most of which look like they've been there just a day too long. Reigning over and above all this, in pride of place, sits the coffee machine. It is treated by the waiters with all the reverence, though perhaps more violence, with which a priest ministers to his altar.

The coffee, in all it's myriad combinations, flows from dawn to dusk, then right round to dawn again. This is the haunt of the builder, sipping his breakfast wine or slugging his mid-morning vermouth, of the housewife, the secretary, the boss, the street cleaner, the gambler, chauffeur, shopper, clubber, everyone, in fact, passes through at some time or other, not least the recently exiled ex-pat.

Many are the sad cases of the English-teaching alcoholic in Spain, the dishevelled, constantly sweaty, red nosed shadow who imparts fidgety knowledge to his students, his eye always on the clock, thinking ahead to his lunchtime drink. It's hardly surprising. So large are the measures, so long are the opening hours, so cheap are the drinks and so convivial are these bars, that anyone with a disposition to addiction will sooner or later fall headlong and helplessly into this sorry state.

That's why I can say, with almost complete certainty, that the addictive trait isn't in me. It was given every possible chance to raise its head. Six nights out of seven during my first year in Spain involved a trip out to the bars of Madrid. There was always someone suggesting a quick drink at the end of the working day, a little huddle in the staff room, eagerly gathering worn-down teachers, minds akimbo from a day's impossible questions and the effort of acting it up, hour after hour, in front of the students. Up the road we would troop, burst into our favourite bar - more wood than zinc, television blaring - and there would be Paco and Ana, open armed, waiting to ply us with cheap beer and plates of free tapas.

'Hi Ana, how are you?'

'Very good.'

'And your boyfriend?'

'Very good. He's had his sperm counted, you know how much he's got?'

'-?'

'Thirty Million!'

'Ah, ...is that good?'

'*Hombre*, it's fantastic!'

'And what about the ants?'

'Still don't believe me eh? There'll be here next week.'

'Yeah, right...'

Ana was a dark, round-faced Colombian girl with a permanent grin and an endless capacity for surprising information. The ants thing came up one night when we asked what they ate in Columbia. Ants' bottoms, she said. Clearly this wasn't to be believed for a minute. So she wrote a letter to a cousin back home, and sure enough, a month later, a tiny Tupperware box arrived, filled with fried, enormous-bottomed ants.

'They're here!' she said one evening.

'Oh God.' There was no way that I was eating one of those giant, freeze-dried genetic mutations.

'Come on, try! Look, delicious.' She popped one into her mouth. *Crunch*.

Paco, the grey-haired true Castillian bar-man in waist-coat and bow tie, was always game for a laugh: *crunch*.

'Just like peanuts,' he said, 'don't be so pathetic.'

'I think I'll just have another beer, thanks.' There are some things you are simply not supposed to put in your mouth.

This hedonistic lifestyle was entirely feasible, as on all but two days of the week I wasn't required to start working until after lunch. Saturday mornings, however, were a calamitous state of affairs. An enormous error in judgment on the part of whoever dictated my timetable had me working Friday nights in a three hour stint until nine, then Saturday mornings at ten. By the end of the evening class on Fridays my capacity for reason was close to melt-down. I would feel withered, withdrawn and incomplete, the victim of those infernal student questions: what's the difference between 'annoyed' and 'upset'? When do you use 'whether' instead of 'if'? Is it 'do you know Madrid?' or 'have you known Madrid?'

Off we would go to the bar, then, it being Friday night, to another, and another, the city's torrid pulse racing through our veins. It was often not until half past four in the morning that I would stumble home, semi-comatose, inches from that four-million-strong urban heart attack, only to appear the following morning as that caricatured, English-teaching alcoholic wreck, in front of a class of twelve bright-eyed students. Stuff it, I thought, barely able to lift myself off my stool and aware that my English was quite possibly worse than theirs, they shouldn't have me working a six day week. And what were these idiots doing here on a Saturday morning anyway? Didn't they go out last night? They, like me, should all be in bed. (Or with me, perhaps, in Nuria's case.)

It's all very well spending your evenings floating amongst the fine variety of drinking establishments in Madrid, spending your days in front of the locals, preaching linguistic doctrines to people who have paid to be converted. But, put simply, a single young man can only take so many exotic young Spanish women in his classes, can only cope for so many Saturday nights amongst the good looking ladies of Madrid, before certain frustrations set in. Or perhaps the word is desires, desires that presented no immediate signs of being fulfilled, not just because I was unable to communicate with any of them, but because I tend to be so shy that I probably wouldn't have done if I could.

What an unfortunate condition! Long gone were my ambitions to wed myself to the French, as were my worries about what would happen to my new dream future wife when she reached the age of her mother. I decided that the shyness thing would have to be overcome when the moment arose, as it inevitably had been in the past, with a good deal of drink and a great deal of patience on the part of the other half. Meanwhile, I set about learning Spanish with a vengeance.

Twice a week I went up to the Spanish department to be force fed verb tables and vocabulary at an alarming rate. This was exactly what I required, and I absorbed everything I could, employing a sort of hierarchical system to select just what I thought I needed to remember next. If, for example, I was taught the word for 'to go shopping', I deemed it to be useful, and into the memory it went (usually to slip out again without me noticing before the next class). If, however, I was presented with a word like 'railing', it would be sidelined until later, when every other word of greater importance had had a chance to be committed to the memory bank. I presume this is a natural system of prioritising language learning, but at the time it seemed revolutionary, and worked a treat. Meanwhile we were being taught a verb tense a week. By the third month we were onto the subjunctives.

The trips up to the top floor were improved no end by the presence of the Spanish Departmental secretary, on whom, like every other man in the building, I had a terrible crush. She had the long, dark Spanish curls, the smooth olive complexion, and her figure, well, she worked part-time as an aerobics instructor.

One day I slipped past as usual, smiling nervously, and went into our classroom. By then we were reduced to myself, another

Englishman called Simon, and Liliana, our wild-haired, forty-something teacher. Twice a week she would breeze in with nothing but a white-board pen, and rustle a lesson out of thin air.

'Good morning *chicos*,' she said, closing the door behind her.

'Morning.'

'I know something about you,' she said, leaning against a table and looking down at me with a smirk on her face.

'What?'

'Well, just maybe a little bird has told me about someone who likes you.'

'What? Who?' I said.

'Well, I'm not sure I'm going to tell you, I mean it's not terribly interesting... but, it could be someone in the Spanish Department.'

'Really? Come on, who is it?' This was inside information that was too good to let go. What if it was that lovely teacher with the short brown hair?

'Well, O.K., I heard that Susanah the secretary thought you were a handsome young man and, what's more, even inquired if you had a girlfriend.'

'What!? You mean...' I nodded towards the door. She was sitting just on the other side of the wall. 'You mean *that* Susanah, the one that sits... No! Impossible!'

'Exactly that Susanah.'

'Wow, mate, well done, she's gorgeous. What are you going to do now?' said Simon, impressed.

'Uh... Oh my God, well, nothing... I don't know.'

'You seem to be going a little red,' said Liliana, 'why don't I go and see if Susanah wants to come in and say hello?'

'What? No, no, thank you, no, please, Liliana wait... What are you doing? *Liliana*...' She was already out of the door. Simon was loving every minute, I was glued to my seat. I could hear them talking outside the door and went into a cold sweat. Any minute now I was going to be subjected to a horrible, crushing humiliation, whereby Liliana would come back with Susanah, the oh-so-sexy Susanah, and they would just stand there and laugh at my innocent stupidity.

Liliana came back in with a text book under one arm, shut the door, and winked at me.

'It's true, you know,' she said, raised her eyebrows in a you-better-believe-it way, then got on with the lesson.

From that day forth I would zip past Susanah's desk, eyes to the floor. What was I going to do? I couldn't possibly say anything to Susanah the secretary! On the occasions when I actually had to sit down and consult her on some administrative matter or other, I would shake so much on the way up the stairs, that by the time I sat down I could hardly speak.

I would lie in bed at night in despair. What was it about these Spanish women that so incapacitated me? It wasn't much good learning how to speak to them if, when the appropriate moment arose, I couldn't actually get any of the words out!

The Lopez sisters, it seemed, held the beginning of the solution to my problems. They were in my fatally-timed Friday-night class, amongst the nicest collection of students I was ever to meet, unspokenly guided by the gentle hand of Professor Benavides, an original Spanish gentleman, whose first words to me were 'It is a very great pleasure to meet you', and whose last, written upon his business card, were 'Thank you for all your kindness'. He arrived each week in a three-piece suit, and brought a paternal warmth to the classes. His enthusiasm never waned, nor did the perpetual arguments with his daughter Catalina, who never ceased to speak Spanish in class, and with whom he always used to sit.

Likewise, the Lopez sisters, twenty-one and twenty-six, always sat together, though so peaceful and good-natured were they that it was a month before it dawned on me that they were actually related. Isabelle, the younger, would slump back with her long legs outstretched, twisting her long black hair round and round in her fingers, whilst Maria, the older, sat bolt-upright, business-like, raising her hand occasionally to offer a half-right answer.

'Do you have an *intercambio*?' asked Isabelle one evening, during the half-time break. We were down in the academy bar, an hour and a half away from freedom.

'No,' I said, 'I don't.'

'Our sister, Eva, is looking for an *intercambio*,' she said, 'would you be interested?'

'Yes', I said, 'definitely.'

Intercambio means an exchange, in this case of languages. As an idea it's simple, effective, brilliant, and why people aren't doing it all over the world is a mystery to me. An English speaker will meet with a Spanish speaker for, say, two hours once a week. An hour will be spent speaking Spanish, the other English. Both parties improve their fluency in the language they are learning and, crucially, have 'real' conversations that you would never get in a classroom.

It's also widely used as a fantastic way of having what is tantamount to an innuendo-free, apparently innocent blind date. So successful, in fact, is this idea of meeting someone of the opposite sex (or sexuality) whilst hiding one's true intentions behind the thinly veiled excuse of learning their language, that some bright entrepreneur started an *intercambio* night club. I went along late one night, purely for research purposes, and was amazed by the depths to which some, less scrupulous 'language learners' had sunk. Everyone wore a label stating their country of origin, and judging by the hi-jinx on display, they weren't too bothered which language they got their practice in. 'Look!' I overheard at the bar, 'Check out Mr Canada trying to get his hand up Italy's skirt!' I never went back after that, especially when I discovered that had I arrived half an hour earlier, I too would have been given a nationality label. Fine, but guess who handed them out at the door? Susanah the secretary.

I met Eva Lopez one night after work. It was raining, late, and Madrid looked like somewhere out of a *noir* fifties detective flick. On the corner where we had arranged to meet stood a tall, slim figure beneath a black umbrella, a tan raincoat falling elegantly away from long, ringlety black curls. Surely, I thought, as I approached the bashful smiling face, the coal-black Spanish eyes, the well balanced cheekbones, surely only in my wildest dreams could this be Eva. My heart had several palpitations, then skipped a few beats. It was.

We talked easily for a couple of hours, she told me how well I spoke Spanish and I complimented her English, which was extremely good. I remember nothing specific, just where we went, one of the awful Irish bars, and the warm glow I felt afterwards. I had spent two hours talking to a Spanish girl, and it felt indescribably good. From then on we met once a week on these terms. I even spent an evening at her house one night, where the collected Lopez sisters fed me up, then took me to the living room and gave me my first taste of dancing Sevillanas. I sat on the sofa watching Eva twirl rhythmically past Isabelle, both with arms held high in the air, neatly sidestepping each other to what sounded like a Far-Eastern Flamenco waltz. I felt extremely contented, and slightly confused.

Would there be something more, I wondered incessantly? She was certainly attractive, forthcoming, always smiling, and never mentioned a boyfriend, but perhaps there was something amiss. While

I waited to see what happened, I kind of hedged my bets. Stephen, friend and partner in *intercambio* crime, had found us a double-*intercambio*-date.

It was disastrous. The pretty one, the air hostess, had little to say, whilst her friend, who was by no means unattractive, wouldn't shut up. She held forth on Buddhism, China and alternative health for an hour and a half once a week for a month, then disappeared to the south coast. There was another, a friend of a different *intercambio* of Stephen's, who I was introduced to one Saturday night. 'This will be your new *intercambio*,' said the mutual friend, though evidently neither of us were very convinced, and I never saw her again.

Meanwhile the Eva situation continued to perplex me. Was she interested? How could I make that *intercambio*/girlfriend conversion, taking the bilingual blind date to its inevitable conclusion, especially when Eva never drank anything but coke?

'Take her to the cinema', advised an ex-pat-expert in the field, 'you know, start doing coupley things,' but I wasn't convinced and never did. The strange weekly conversation sessions continued as before.

Meanwhile frustration, desire, and the sheer good fun of it all, catapulted me on every feasible occasion around the innumerable bars of Madrid.

≈

A class was forced upon me one hazy Friday morning in February, not six months after my arrival in Spain. A teacher was ill, and I was on 'standby'. The group in question was rumoured to be impossible to control and I was relieved when twenty minutes into the class no-one had turned up. I'll give them 10 more minutes I thought, then I'm off. Then a girl appeared, apologised for being late and sat in a chair up against the back wall. I pulled my stool into the middle of the room, sat down in front of her and we talked. She was, I remember, very friendly. She knew England, had even been to Oxford, where I grew up. Her English was good. Soon her classmates arrived in dribbles, practically rioted for two hours, then left. Another standby completed, albeit an unusual one. My powers of class control, not least my nerves, had been stretched to the limits. Nothing else. Not yet.

Chinese Meals and Flat Cats

From my early wanderings about Madrid, two observations repeatedly struck me. Firstly, that there was no river, and secondly, that there were no coloured people, that Madrid was almost exclusively populated by Spaniards.

On the first count I was wrong, at least partially. Madrid does indeed have a river, the Manzanares, although it is more of a dirty little canal than a *rio*, borders a six lane ring-road, and is an embarrassment to the city's population. On the second count, however, I was somewhat nearer the mark. In the final years of the twentieth century, Madrid was anything but a multiracial metropolis.

What immigrant population existed was largely South American, though at first I failed to notice this as they also spoke in Spanish. But there were blatantly no Africans, barely any Asians, and all but a scattering of other Europeans. All those that hadn't been extricated several centuries ago by the Inquisition had, I imagined, been kicked out by General Franco, and practically no-one was being let back in. All this, of course, with the exception of the Chinese.

There has long been a large, well established Chinese population in Spain. Though they integrate little with the Spanish on a personal level, they operate extensive import and wholesale networks, own excellent cheap convenience food stores, and run curious Chinese restaurants. Glance into any, from Madrid to Malaga, Toledo to Torremolinos, and you will notice that the waiters and waitresses have suspiciously little to do. Whilst the rough-round-the-edges, rubbish-on-floor Spanish bar does a roaring trade in canned starters and fried sardines, again, the staff of two in the Chinese restaurant next door are loitering around the front desk with nothing to do. The food is no worse than that being dished up by their countrymen in London, Paris or Berlin, and provides incredibly good value for money, yet these restaurant are rarely even half-full.

There are two simple reasons for this. Firstly, the Spanish are the most insular, single-mindedly passionate devotees to their own national cuisine. Secondly, malicious rumours are afoot. It is said, by some of the Spanish at least, that in Spain the Chinese never die. At least not officially. They simply regenerate. The identity of the deceased - passports, papers and so on - is somehow transferred onto a newcomer from China, thus bypassing immigration problems and ensuring that the Chinese population is constantly refreshed. To the suspicious Spanish mind, this leaves an obvious problem with the disposal of the dead relative, who must be 'disappeared' unofficially and inconspicuously: sweet and sour, sir, or black bean sauce?[1]

Had I known this at the time then it is unlikely that I would have been sitting in a Chinese restaurant in Cuenca one bitter November evening, and even less likely that I would have turned down the vegetarian dishes and plumped, hungrily, for the chicken. Al and I were on a photographic weekend, and we were out celebrating a momentous decision: that sooner or later we would have our first exhibition.

I had met Al, a fellow teacher, at the academy where we both worked. With three years in the country already behind him, he was an excellent guide in those early days to the ways of Spain. Just thirty, from Malvern, his close-shaven haircut and earrings hid a quick wit and easy-going ideas. We discovered a mutual interest beyond the bars of Madrid: photography. It was soon decided that a photographic trip was in order at the first available opportunity.

Cuenca, not two hours from Madrid, was near enough to allow me to work my Saturday morning shift, and still let us arrive for the last hours of daylight. The bus ride southeast had me glued to the window. Previously I had made brief Sunday visits to the nearby cities of Segovia, that frozen granite masterpiece shivering peacefully behind the Sierra de Guadarrama, and Aranjuez, so full of tall leafless trees, damp grey skies and broad, suited men with well wrapped-up wives, that it looked like autumnal England a generation ago.

Cuenca, however, existed alone, far from the grip of the capital, deep in Castilla la Mancha: Don Quijote territory. The city lies at the end of a long twisting highway that passes nowhere else on the way, and appears to go nowhere else afterwards. There, at the highest point of a precipitous river cliff, cut off on either side by two great ravines, is the old town, an urban carbuncle set hard against bitter winds in winter and unbearable heat in summer. Right at the top is a

---

[1] When the squirrel population recently disappeared from Madrid's Retiro park, the Chinese and their strange culinary habits were immediately thought to be number one suspects.

lofty plaza, where a lonely tower lets out a desperate wail of bells every half an hour.

After our supper we headed out to see how Cuenca's *marcha*, night life, compared to that in Madrid. Having wandered around for some time in search of the city's youth, we were on the point of giving up when we spotted some steps descending between two buildings on the edge of the main square. There at the bottom a tiny crowded plaza hung dramatically above the dark ravine, the new town's lights glittering far below. This is where they were hiding.

In a cluster of bars that lined the plaza music roared whilst the masses outside fought their way in to buy beer in litre bottles. When later everyone moved down to the new town we went with them, to a tiny street consisting of nothing but more bars, raucous energy and the bitter cold. We talked to anyone who would listen, and tried hard to talk to those, mostly girls, that wouldn't. For example:

Setting: disco/drinking bar.

Our ploy: two innocent English boys who don't speak Spanish.

(*Off-handed approach to two local girls standing by the dance floor.*)

Us: Hello.

Girls: *Hola.*

(*Pause, smiles.*)

Girls, aside: *Estan intentando ligar con nosotras.*

Me: What did they say?

Al: That we're trying to get off with them.

Girls (with ploy of own): Buy us a drink.

Us: No.

Girls: Goodbye.

When at last everyone went to the disco down the road, along we went too, until finally, at half past six in the morning, we were politely asked to leave, though I don't remember why.

We spent Sunday taking photographs, spurred on by *carajillos*, a cure-all coffee and cognac combination we drank to ward off the cold, hangovers, and fatigue. We wandered up the river below the cliffs until the town disappeared entirely at a bend in the road, where tall calligraphic trees reached out to the rocky escarpments above. Life was fantastic, Spain was fantastic, Cuenca was the greatest place on earth and as for our exhibition, well that was going to be momentous. My God those *carajillos* were good. We summited the old town again, ran around up there then raced back down, until, just as the sun was setting, having been chased off railway land by an over-insistent gypsy who lived in a shack, we got the bus back to Madrid.

I was hooked, on wild landscapes and a rhythm of life previously unknown. I knew then that I simply wanted to wander around, with or without the camera, just to wander around in these landscapes. Somehow or other, no matter how long it took, I would have to see all of Spain.

≈

Soon after the return from Cuenca, I left Eduardo's flat. I like to think that it had nothing to do with that short story he left lying around, the one about mediaeval cannibals and nasty scenes of dismemberment. I just realised that however princely my accommodation above the Plaza Mayor was, I was essentially sleeping in his living room, and what's more, paying three times the going rental-rate for the privilege. That was money that could be far better spent on trips around the country. Besides this, I had been awoken every single Sunday by the Plaza's latest event. One week it was the healthy-heart fair, the next the last leg of the Spanish cycling tour. Whatever it was, a man with enormous capacity to make noise was handed a microphone and encouraged to start shouting through it from eight o'clock in the morning.

I looked into the small ads of the local papers and discovered three possible shared flats. The first I couldn't find. The second turned out to be shared with an entire extended family from Ecuador. The third sounded promising. 'Who lives there?' I got Al to ask her on the phone. 'Just a dentist, no-one else,' she said, so he told her that I would come and have a look.

I stood on the three-lane thoroughfare outside her front door thinking that this certainly didn't tally with the peace and quiet mentioned in the ad. But if I didn't ring the bell and I didn't have a look, then I would incur bad flat-hunting Karma, and that would be that.

She buzzed me up the stairs. My first glance over her shoulder revealed that she had lied, that this was blatantly her flat, in which she obviously still lived as well. The twee furnishings and carefully arranged ornaments matched the silvery hair tied up in a bun, her soft wrinkles and neat pinny. I shouldn't have rung the bell, I thought, I knew I shouldn't have rung!

Once I had been shown my room, the crochéd bed cover and reading lamp type that you find in B and B's, once we had seen the dentist's room, her room, and were standing in her quaintly cosy living room, I turned my attention to the cat, a wary Siamese. I was biding my time until I could escape. Say hello to the cat, I thought, then say goodbye. I bent down to stroke it.

Whoosh! In a flash I had the thing hanging from my forearm by four razor-clawed paws and one set of teeth. It just hung there, swinging, growling savagely while I looked down in horror and turned white. The old woman, as if this happened all the time, flew into a frenzy of cursing and screaming and whipped at the cat with a tea towel she had untucked from her belt.

'*Madre Mia! Madre Mia! Que Gato!*' she screamed, '*Este maldito gato, que voy a hacer, Madre Mia que gato!*'

Why won't it let go, I thought, it's stuck on my arm - what's going on and why, why, why? She kept on whipping away and swearing and screeching until at last, with my bloody arm at chest level, the cat let go and fell to the floor.

I stood in a state of shock, dripping blood onto the frayed carpet while she set about the cat again with the tea-towel, it never retreating more than a metre or two before darting towards me again as if to make a fresh attack.

'Um... a little water, please?' I said, holding my arm up at her. She disappeared out of the room, leaving me with the spitting, rasping cat, reappearing a moment later with medical alcohol, then ushering me towards the bathroom, the cat close behind, tea-towel blows still flying. As I cleaned myself up in the sink, one eye on the blasted animal, she stood her ground beside me and regained her composure. Then, quite suddenly, with all the flair of the oiliest estate agent, she flung an arm towards the bath.

'And *this*', she said, 'is the bathroom. Complete with hot *and* cold water shower.'

On the way out, by some inexplicable act of politeness, I thought that I had better take a final look at the room, to make her feel like there was still a chance that I might take it after all. The old lady waited by the front door with a look of defeat on her face. She knew the game was up, that the pet thing had blown it again. The traffic roared beneath the bedroom window. I noticed that since I had first looked around the room, a large yellow damp patch had appeared on the pillow. The cat jumped down off the bed, smiling, and through muffled growls and whines, saw me out of the flat.

I gave up on the small ads. The renting situation in Spain is quite different to that in England because the young simply don't want, can't afford or aren't allowed to flee the nest. Until they get married or get kicked out, somewhere approaching the age of thirty, they remain living with the family, even though they might have a good job with a very reasonable salary. This money they prefer to save until the time comes to move into a bought flat with their new spouse. There are of course restrictions to living out your wild years with your parents, but there are ways around that. I once crossed a vast empty parking lot one afternoon on the outskirts of Barcelona. At first I couldn't work out why every few yards I had to avoid treading on used condoms. There is still one thing that a very real majority of Spanish youngsters are forced to do for the first time in a car, somewhere out of the way, on some furtive moonless night.

The upshot of this is that young people rarely live in shared flats. Even during university they will stay at home, as, like the French, they all study their degree in their home town. The only rooms that come up for rent tend to be with either the unmarried over-thirty year old who's looking for company, or the very rooms that are left vacant in their wake. The parents see a way to capitalise on the 'child's' removal, and put the room up for rent. I didn't want to live with either the parents or the boring thirty year old. For a while it looked like Eduardo and I were stuck with each other.

Then Barbara, a Scottish girl who had been on the September teaching course, came to the rescue. Having experienced exactly the same problems she suggested that we look for an empty flat to share. Within a week she had found a two-bedroom third-floor place roughly the size of Eduardo's living room. By a miracle of architectural contortionism it somehow contained a kitchen, a bathroom and enough shared space for a sofa, an armchair and an outsized, outdated television. All this and a bedroom each for less than a hundred quid a month. Now provisioned with an adequate base, there was plenty of time to continue the exploration of Spain.

As for Eduardo, I saw him a year and a half later, dressed in a sharp grey suit in a night club in San Sebastian.

'I don't work in the Hostel anymore,' he said, and then, growling Al Pacino-style, 'Now, I'm a *Businessman*!'

16th June 2001

These days I live in a flat in the old barrio, or neighbourhood, of Lavapies, ten minutes south of the Puerta del Sol, the absolute centre of Madrid. I come home for lunch via Tirso de Molina metro, only because it's downhill from there to my flat, a necessity in this weather. Hunched up at the bottom of the stairs that climb from the metro's grimy mouth to the dazzling light in the plaza, is a leather-clad youth calling, 'Preservativos! Cien pesetas!' He is holding out a long string of stolen or faulty vending-machine condoms. I can't imagine for a minute who would risk using one, even at a hundred pesetas a bundle.

At the top of the steps as usual is the grizzled man with the blaring radio in his pocket, doing a blisteringly slow trade in counterfeit batteries. I presume that the untuned, unintelligible radio is there to remind us what the batteries are for. His face is clenched as tight as the ribs of a barrel, battened down against the ferocious attack of the sun. It is June, and to everyone's surprise high summer has arrived with a bang: de golpe. It came one afternoon last week, needling its way through the tight streets, a fiery thread weaving a blanket of heat so intense that it will stifle and suffocate us remorselessly for the next three months. Already we have seen forty degrees. '¡Ayyy - Que Calor!', what heat, moans the city weakly and in unison, when only last week we were busy complaining bitterly about the cold ('¡Ayyyy - Que FRIO! ¡Brrr....!')

In the middle of the plaza, the old playwright Tirso de Molina stands on his pedestal, condemned in granite to gaze forever upon the gangs of drunks that have taken refuge in the shade of the scattered trees. Twenty years ago, before the Mayor came and turfed them all out, the square was full of artists who made a living selling their work to the tourists. Now, despite the striking, bright yellow old apartments, it's just a dusty drinking spot, littered with cans and wandering dogs, and stinking of piss.

Two streets lead down from the Plaza into the barrio of Lavapies. I take Calle de Jesus y Maria, turning past the old sailor in charge of the cars outside Asador Fronton, the famous brassery on the

45

corner. He sits on someone's bonnet, propped up on two sticks, chewing his teeth and hissing, 'tsss... tsss... Eh...Guapa!' to the occasional passing beauty.

The road plunges quickly away from the sunlight of the Plaza, the irregular line of tall, fused buildings descending like a shady tree-lined path into woodland. Down past the piercing parlour whose shadowy half-shuttered interior transfixes a huddle of teenage girls, their crop-tops revealing tight bellies and olive skin, exposed for imminent perforation. They bow their heads as I pass, a huddle of wary whisperers, as if mother were just about to storm around the corner and drag them back to their senses.

Then there's the view along Calle Calvario, one of Old Madrid's finest in summer, its converging lines of nineteenth-century apartment blocks bathed in blinding light, tall windows etched into sandy facades. Heading on, past the low, first-floor balconies whose potted firs level with wrought-iron wall lamps, l catch first sight of the trees at the bottom, a vast, sea-green canopy sailing gently in the breeze. There at last, amongst the humid voices that ripple between the benches, beneath the cool umbrella of shade, I reach my building's front door.

I throw open the balcony doors and eat alone, perching among the sparrows, four floors up in the tree tops, sharing my meal with the ambling clutter of noises, the aromas of fried fish and olive oil, that rise through branches and leaves from the pavement below.

The Ecstasy of Travel

'The purpose of travel being to obtain ecstasy - that delight which one had as a child but lost later - I had it here.' So says Gerald Brenan in '*The Face of Spain*.' He was sitting by a brown stony river near Malaga, looking at a line of trees, and beyond, to a distant mountain. Nothing else. That is the essence of Spain, the profound effect of a simple landscape.

At Easter I spent a week in the southern province of Andalucia, crossing such landscapes with Stephen and Mark, a visiting friend from England. We drove over mountains that could have been flown in from Peru, swam off a tropical beach at the Cape of Trafalgar, where the Atlantic keeps the Mediterranean hemmed in, sat upon the great dune at Bolonia watching Morrocan towns glowing like fireflies across the glassy straights, and in white-washed hill-top villages witnessed processions of such religious devotion and imagination that you would be hard pressed to see something more impressive anywhere in the world today.

While we were there we had a quick bash at putting our *intercambio* skills to the test. Sitting on a stony beach at Almuñeca one night, taking a break from a dreadful teeny disco, we spotted three girls of our age sitting a little further along the shore.

'Right,' said Stephen, 'I'm going for a piss. If you two aren't talking to those girls by the time I get back, I give up.' Stephen had already discovered that neither Mark nor I were very good at talking to unknown women, Mark because he didn't speak a word of Spanish, was happily engaged and had no desire to *intercambio* anything with anyone, and me because, well, same problems as always.

'O.K., we'll show him,' I said to Mark, as Stephen strode off up the beach. Fortified by a couple of gin and tonics, we wandered sheepishly over to the three girls.

'*Hola, sabeis donde esta la marcha por aqui?*'' That old chestnut, did they know where to go out around here.

So, by the time Stephen did get back, a bemused look on his face, everything was going swimmingly. I was sitting next to a pretty blond girl from Vallecas (I was sure that this was a dodgy part of

Madrid, but was prepared to let this pass), and Mark was putting up with some dreadful English from the other two. Pretty soon we had agreed to head back to the teeny disco for a drink. Forget Eva, I thought, things are looking interesting in Almuñeca. At least they were for a while. So impressed was I that this Spanish girl was spending so much time talking to me, that I decided a constant stream of gin and tonics would be required to get me through to the end.

It must have been when I started having trouble constructing even simple sentences in Spanish that a stormy look settled upon her face. A few minutes later she just gave up and went over to talk to her friends. One thing that very rarely goes down well in Spain is blatant inebriation.

An hour or so later we walked them back to the old town, where we were all staying. Where Stephen and I had failed, Mark was battling away with the third of the friends.

'Come on, come for a walk on the beach with me,' she said.

'No, I can't, I'm engaged,' said Mark.

'Come on, it doesn't matter,' she grabbed his arm, he pulled it away.

'Look, I'm in love with my girlfriend.'

'Well, give me your telephone number.'

'I live in England for goodness sake!'

A month later I was in Andalucia again, this time in Granada. I arrived one Friday night at half past four in the morning and was greeted by Al, who had got there the day before. Should we have one quick drink, or go to bed, to be fresh for the following day?

One quick drink. An hour later we were in a bar dug into a hill in the Sacremonte quarter. A guitar passed from hand to hand as local musicians took it in turns to strum out wild Flamenco beats, their gravelly voices wrestling with improvised tales of heart-break. Young couples danced, hands clapped in skipping triplets, jokes flew back and forth. When at last we emerged from the hillside we made our way through the narrow maze of flower-decked, tight white streets in the Albaicin until, as if by a miracle, we came out at the Mirador de San Nicolas.

Here, with the empty, leafy plaza, a small church and the sunrise at our backs, we sat on a wall high above Granada and watched the slow illumination of the Alhambra Palace, her ruddy walls steeped in mist from the cascading, olive-green vegetation that tumbles from the ramparts to the valley below. Beyond, the snowy peaks of the

Sierra Nevada slowly rose from the haze, cutting a meek horizon into the morning sky.

Beware 'one quick drink' in Granada. We finally went to bed half an hour before midday. A few hours later we awoke, grabbed our cameras and rushed into the old town. It was Las Cruces festival, the reason we had come to Granada in the first place. Whilst we slept the town had been transformed. Plazas that had been empty in the small hours were now swarming with people, with most of the activity surrounding *chiringuitos*, makeshift market-stall bars. These mainly traded in a local drink known as *calicasas*, a lethal mixture of vermouth and various unidentified liquors. Laid out along the bar tops were plates of long, earthy broad beans, which one podded oneself and chewed between drinks.

Each plaza also contained a blaring sound system, belting out chart-topping Spanish pop and traditional Sevillanas, and, set up in each corner, a large cross made of flowers, the *cruces* after which the fiesta takes its name. In front of these, small children danced to the music on raised wooden platforms, dressed up like their parents - colourful polka-dot frocks for the girls and tight grey suits for the boys. At the edge of the plazas men in wide-rimmed black hats sat bolt upright on elegant horses, their wives sitting side-saddle, tucked up close behind.

'That's the posh lot that ride in from the villages outside town,' said Al, 'all the rich families in the country around here own horses.' Al had lived in Granada for a year and constantly regretted having left. It was only the lack of regular work that had reluctantly driven him to move to Madrid. 'Come on,' he said 'let's go and get a drink.'

We spent what was left of the afternoon wandering around the cobbled streets and crowded plazas, drinking *calicasas* and taking photographs. I felt deliriously happy. For someone who grew up in an English village where the local fiesta was an afternoon flower show whose highlight was the largest vegetable competition, these contented dancing masses were a revelation. The only remote resemblance I could see between Las Cruces and my old village fete were the plates of broad beans.

As dusk fell we found ourselves by the fountain in the Plaza Nueva, dancing beneath the palm trees with two beautiful girls from the university.

'Why are you here?' shouted the first above the music.

'We live in Madrid,' I replied, 'we've come for the weekend to see Las Cruces.'

'Do you like it?'

'It's wonderful!'

'Can you dance Sevillanas?'

'No,' I said, 'but Al can.'

'Come on then!' she said, and when the music changed and the wild, flamenco-esque Sevillanas started up, she and Al twirled around in time to the four set parts of the dance.

'Now you learn,' she said when they had finished, 'just copy me!'

And as the music began she stared into my eyes and stepped first back, then forward, then spun around, and I tried my best to follow her but was lost at every turn, and I didn't care at all because all I could think was 'here I am, dancing around with this gorgeous Andalucian medical student, in this unbelievable town in the south of Spain - sod England, and the Radley Flower show, I'm staying here forever!' We danced with the girls and occasionally went to the bar and revelled in it all until of course we had one *calicasas* too many and the girls, who saw we were drunk, made polite excuses and quickly disappeared.

'Pah! Who cares,' said Al, 'do you want to see the most beautiful street in the world?'

I followed him to the head of the square, where a simple church marked the start of a narrow cobbled street, the Carrera del Darro. Three storey stone buildings lined one side, interrupted occasionally by narrow alleyways that disappeared uphill into the labyrinth lanes of the Albaicin. On the other, a low wall ran above a gentle stream several metres below, from which vast quantities of vegetation rose to street level, palm fronds vying for space with extravagant grasses and small trees bearing curious fruits. Birds darted amongst the branches and a broken Roman bridge jutted out from between two houses on the opposite bank, its disrupted path suspended in mid air. We reached a narrow plaza, and above, high on a bluff, the flood-lit walls of the Alhambra glowed orange in the dark. Here the street ended, and just where the stream disappeared off into the fields beyond stood the largest fig tree I had ever seen, a luxuriant, burgeoning mass of deep green leaves and fruit, a giant guarding the city limits, fingers gently trailing in the water at its feet.

'Yes,' I said, 'this really is the most amazing street in the world.'

But neither this, nor any of the extraordinary Andalucian landscapes I had seen before, have stuck in my mind like that first view of the Alhambra Palace from the Mirador de St Nicolas at dawn. It is a view that you might stumble across on any day of the week, yet something, the quality of light at that moment, the simplicity of the elements - the misty, cascading vegetation, the auburn palace walls, the mountains rising behind - had made the scene quite magnificent. Perhaps it was Brenan's ecstasy of travel, and the child in me seeking it out.

≈

From these and other trips our first exhibition emerged at last. Al and I had joined up with two more photographers, Jackie and Matt, to form a group dubbed '*Extranjeros* (foreigners) Out of Focus'. We met once a week, looked at some slides, told each other what great photographers we were, then went out for 'one quick drink'. The academy had agreed to let us use the walls in their foyer and bar area for a month, and to hold a private view in April, our big night.

It was, if the warning we got afterwards was anything to go by, a significantly bigger night than any of us had expected, or actually remembered. The following day the supreme director motioned us into a quiet office and interrogated us about raucous behaviour, wild drunkenness and inadequate cleaning. He reminded us that the country's leading political party headquarters were only just round the corner, and it wouldn't do much good if they thought that any untoward behaviour was afoot in our highly respected teaching establishment.

Obviously he had been totally misinformed. True enough the bar-man was doing a sneaky sideline in double-measure gin and tonics, and the most senior member of staff present did lose his footing momentarily on the stairs by the lavatories, but there was none of the drunken nonsense associated with normal staff events (karaoke, over-sexed fancy dress and over play of Abba's greatest hits, that sort of thing). What's more, for the first time in its history, we had actually made the place look rather nice. Jackie exhibited prints from her travels in Africa, Matt from his wanders about Madrid, Al and I from our trips around Spain. The most talked about piece was undoubtedly

Al's 'Dead Dog'. This was a closely-cropped, rather forensic shot of the amputated back half of a canine that we had found one afternoon in some scrub-land outside Hoyo de Manzanares, a commuter town to the north of Madrid.

Everyone we could think of was invited, all of our students, even the chatterbox Buddhist *intercambio*. She lectured me on photography for an hour, then left. The whole thing passed off without a hitch. It was liquid, certainly, though by no means drunken, and as far as we know the political party down the road never had us down as a serious security risk. The four of us swanned around bathing in momentary glory, practically famous in fact, and to top it all I even sold a print. It portrayed a distorted cream-coloured church tower, reflected upside down in river water, but exhibited the right way up again: a simple trick. I had taken it months before on a cold Sunday morning in Cuenca, as Al and I wandered hungover along a ravine, joking about the idea we had had the night before, that one day we might actually get round to having an exhibition.

24th June 2001

It is five a.m., maybe nearer to six. I always wake up at this time. It's silent outside, and I imagine that it must be this that wakes me, or is it the drop in temperature at night? It's nearing the end of June, and we have to sleep with the windows open. They have been open since the end of May... I must get on tomorrow if I'm to finish this in time... The silence outside is surely what woke me up. Up here in the trees we escape some of the noise. But even when it is 'quiet' during the day, there is always the chatter of voices, or the fluttering song of a caged bird.

And there is a good deal of violent noise. The drunks, singing or shouting when it's far too late. The bin-men who come every night of the week at half past one - now I only hear them if I'm still awake. And the cars who are blocked into the garage just up the road, that hoot and hoot until the guilty party comes and removes his car. They hoot at any hour, but at least they have a reason, unlike the hooters who sit on their horns right below our windows just because they have to wait two minutes while someone unloads at the shop down the road. It makes you want to shoot them, somewhere really painful, or at least to throw an egg or two.

Finally, there is the soft noise, whose dream-like quality is welcome at any time of day or night. Those poor caged birds. The pianist up the street. The knife sharpener, who pushes his special bicycle with grindstones on the handlebars up the street, and announces his arrival by blowing a twist of notes from a wooden whistle that he raises again and again to his lips. He could have been wandering these streets for hundreds of years. And sometimes, when I awake at five a.m. or six, there is one permissible noise that still counts as silence, the sound of the cleaning men with the hoses, who come in the night to water the streets.

Olive Bones

One hot Friday night in May, Al, Stephen, some of our students and I, were standing in the Fino Bar, one of the finest bars in Madrid. The capital, being the sum of its nation's parts, allows you to eat or drink in a different province every night of the week. An Asturian bar one night, a Basque restaurant the next. At weekends we always made a quick trip to this bar, to pure Andalucia.

We were squashed up into one corner drinking *Fino*, the powerful sherry which always guarantees a wild evening and a desperate hang-over the following day. The bar, small, rectangular, sawdust on the tiled floor, two chorizo sausages and a slightly sorry looking leg of ham hanging on one wall, was packed. Two girls danced exaggeratedly to the constant Sevillanas music blasting out from a cheap stereo, whilst the crowd spurred them on with hand claps, and the bar-men beat time between swigs of *Fino* with a 'clackety clickety click' from a split bamboo stick. Occasionally the Sevillanas would stop abruptly and what sounded like an upbeat Flamenco-fied children's song would come on. Then everyone would wave their bottles of *Fino* in the air and sing so loudly that it looked like the place would burst at the seams.

Amidst all this an olive bone, a *hueso de acietuna*, what we call the stone, flew over some heads, tapped me on the shoulder and landed at my feet. Another flew wide and failed to hit its mark. Someone was trying to catch my attention. I didn't notice a thing, but turned to try and fight my way to the bar. Another bottle was required. I squeezed forward past a huddle of friends then stopped short, my path blocked by cropped black hair, honey-hazel eyes, and an impossibly radiant smile.

'*¿Eres Ben, no?*' You're Ben aren't you?

'Yes,' I replied, shouting above the noise, trying to place the face, '....and who are you?'

'My name is Marina,' she said, 'you taught me English one morning a few months ago when my teacher was ill. I think I was the first to arrive.'

'Yes, I remember, you'd been to Oxford. You're from the crazy group.'

'No, not so crazy. What are you doing here?'

'Well, I'm just here with some friends, some students,' I said.

'Your Spanish is good, isn't it?'

'Is it? Thank you!'

'Do you have an *intercambio*?'

This was an interesting question. I thought briefly of Eva, hesitated, then lied.

'No, no I don't actually, well I mean I did, but now I don't... anymore. And you?'

She wrote her number on the back of a local train timetable, I promised to phone, and pressed on to the bar.

Bottle in hand, I pushed my way back to our corner.

'Eh Ben! You're not allowed to *ligar* with your students you know,' said Maria-Jesus.

'No, no, she's not a student, she's just into doing an *intercambio*.'

'Ha! We know what that means!'

We polished off the bottle, I waved goodbye to Marina, and we forced our way out of the bar. The streets of Alonso Martinez were thronging, thick crowds of happy people drifting up and down, leaning on car bonnets, drinking on corners, piling in and out of the bars. The easy ebbs and flows of a typical Friday night in Madrid, not a hint of the antagonism or violence you might sense in British towns in that balmy summer air, just a simple disposition to excitement, to enjoyment, to seeing what might happen from one moment to the next.

I phoned Marina two days later. We arranged to meet on Thursday. Four days of nerves and desperate attempts to resurrect a clear picture of her from beneath the *Fino* haze were banished in an instant when she strolled up to me outside the academy, kissed me on each cheek, and said:

'*Hola! Que Cuentas?*' Literally: Hello, what do you tell?

We made our way to the Cervezeria Santa Barbara, where my grandfather had drunk whilst on business in Madrid fifty years before. It probably hasn't changed since. Amongst the long wooden tables and the happy din of tired professionals one day away from their weekend, we talked easily and drank glasses of beer. There was none of the uncertainty of the old *intercambios*, no awkward pauses, nor the obviously forced questions that English teachers keep prepared for untalkative classes. We moved on to the Cafe Belen, a candle-lit place tucked down a side street that played music you might hear in fashionable London bars, in surroundings that belonged in France: dated, marble cafe tables, art on the walls, dried grasses in the corners, flowers on the bar in a tall glass vase. Sitting at the big oak table in the corner, we tossed peanuts onto its glass top, marking out imaginary journeys on the old map that was pinned out below.

I walked her home along the Paseo de Prado, past the famous museum and the statue of Velazquez, brushes in hand, reclined in his sturdy bronze chair, then past the succulent scents seeping through the railings of the botanical gardens. Here, to shatter the romantic allusions, we stopped opposite MacDonalds, planted kisses on each cheek, arranged to meet the following Thursday, and went our separate ways.

'How was it?' asked Barbara as I raced through the door.

'Better than Eva.'

I fell into bed feeling incredibly content, ecstatic even and, as usual, confused.

Meanwhile, to further confound things, the academic year was drawing to a close. I had declined to renew my contract for the following year on various grounds. That such an exhausting timetable didn't fit in with my original aims (what were they anyway? To concentrate on photography?). That I refused to work a six day week or a Saturday morning ever again. Because I met a woman on the Eurostar on my first journey to Madrid who told me that on no account should I teach for more than a year. Because I still wanted to go and live by the sea (I still do). I didn't really know what I would do. There seemed to be a sort of void ahead as empty and uncertain as the previous nine months had been unexpected and self-perpetuating. To cap things off I had also told Barbara that I would be leaving the flat at the end of July, and she had promised my room to someone else. I had no clear options in mind, not even the fanciful or ridiculous 'marry a French girl' type this time. If it wasn't for my new *intercambio* and the prospect of another exhibition, I might have started to panic.

By the beginning of June I had seen Marina three times, each better than the last, each distinctly innocent, exciting, and frustrating as I burst into the flat to tell Barbara how it had gone. Or hadn't. At least the *Extranjeros* Out of Focus were swinging into action again. We had managed to secure wall space in July at the very same Cafe de Belen, and went along one night to show Pablo, the owner, what we wanted to put on display. Eva had been in touch unexpectedly so I brought her along too. She was on radiant form and *intercambio*'d happily away with all of us as I showed Pablo my sepia sand prints, Al produced his distorted portraits, Jackie her black and white doors, and Matt, well Matt still hadn't sorted his out yet.

Pablo was a tall, bright eyed aesthete with gaunt features and the ability to look both enthusiastic and withdrawn at the same time. It was impossible to tell how old he was, either thirty- or forty-something, depending on the angle from which you looked at him. He flicked slowly through our work, judging each photograph with the quiet consideration of an expert trying to spot a fake. To our surprise we convinced him of our authenticity, and he announced in a soft, amused voice that he was pleased. A date was set for the private view, our next night of fame, the 5th of July.

'Eva's a nice girl,' they all said afterwards.

'Don't', I replied, 'not now!'

The following Thursday I met Marina again. We walked through the city to a Galician Bar, El Gallego, in the close-knit quarter of Santo Domingo. The Galician effect was so authentic - with the trays of prawns and octopus, doorstep slices of pepper and chorizo *tortilla,* and the smell of sweet fermented grape - that you could almost imagine walking out later into some blustery north-western seaport. Almost, if it hadn't been for the heat. The walls were too warm to lean on, the air too hot to stand in. We drank a bottle of cloudy Ribeiro wine in defiance of it, out of small white china bowls. Then we drank another.

Stumbling, reeling, swimming through the impossible warmth, we set out across the city again. We found ourselves in La Latina, climbed the stairs to the roof-terrace bar of El Viajero, and sat at a table looking across to the broad dome of the Basilica de San Francisco. We ordered a beer each, just to make sure, and swayed towards each other on our bar stools. Still nothing happened.

We set off again, but this time in the direction of Marina's house, as it was obvious that neither of us could take anything more to drink. A dreadful countdown had begun. Every step led us closer to her door, a step towards the non-resolution of the same old problem. Half-way there and still nothing, I racked my brains, what should I do? She had decided that I couldn't be interested and had given up all hope. On we went, resigned to our misfortunes, until suddenly, just outside the Reina Sofia Museum I grabbed her arm, we stumbled headlong towards each other, and ended up propped against a wall, kissing clumsily in a drunken embrace.

The temperatures increased gradually as June drew to a close. Every day someone would come into the staff room with a record sighting from one of the thermometer clocks that stand about the city on iron stalks. One day I spotted 48 degrees, which was both extremely doubtful and wholly reasonable. It was blisteringly hot. It made you feel alive, then it made you feel sick, and always it made you tired. Ice creams had to be bought and eaten in air conditioned buildings and no-one, not even the Spanish, walked on the sunny side of the street.

The *intercambios* with Marina stopped being strictly *intercambios* and became far more frequent. The school term, my last, crawled to a melting halt. There was a leaving dinner, where I was presented with a book.

≈

Jono, an old friend, arrived from England. We had hatched a plan during the year to cross half the Pyrenees by foot. A route existed, the GR11, and he had a book breaking the entire range down into day walks with descriptions like: 'An easy day's ascent', or 'A challenging day with possibility of mountaineering diversions'. What qualified us in our minds as mountain men was our record in the field of adventurous pursuits. Two years before we had cycled through Normandy for five days, averaging 40 miles a day, camping at night, and carrying all our provisions. I returned to England barely able to walk. The year after that we had attempted to cycle the Thames Path from London to Oxford, probably the bumpiest, most rutted and least maintained cycle path in Europe. After two days of non-stop jolts and one equally uncomfortable night, we skipped off the path at Wallingford, and did the rest by road. Now we hoped to walk consecutively for eighteen days across terrain that started at about 2,500 metres, and ended at San Sebastian on the Basque coast. No problem. It was all laid out in the book, day by day, contour by contour.

With five days to go until the opening night of the second exhibition, we decided to head off to the Picos de Europa for some training: compass practice, breaking in our boots, that sort of thing. The 'Picos' are a mini mountain range cast onto the Northern shores of

Spain, in the province of Asturias. They rise from the plains behind so abruptly and sit so tight against the coastline in front, that I imagine some divine cartographer had only left them there momentarily by mistake. The inhabitants of this magical world survive on boisterous stews of beans and sausage, and live a largely pastoral life, still cutting hay from steep slopes with scythes, and collecting it with pitch forks.

We drove up to Caen, a tiny hamlet hemmed in on all sides by near vertical pastures, tumbling streams and razor-sharp limestone peaks. The setting was impressively remote and whether terrifyingly beautiful, or beautifully terrifying, I couldn't decide. The cool climate proved a perfect antidote to the extremes of Madrid, like swallowing a bottle of oxygen and climbing into the fridge. We put up our tent in a field by a stream and later an old man trailing a bushel of tree branches came past and collected our rent, about a pound.

Early the next morning we started into the mighty Cares Gorge, an eight mile, twisting ravine whose tight sheer walls often measure a thousand metres from top to bottom. A well cut path follows its length at vertiginious heights, designed to follow and allow maintenance access to a swift waterway that rises and falls, gurgling away beside you, built to deliver power to a hydro electric scheme in a village at the other end.

For four hours you walk, pinned to the sides of this abyss, passed only by the occasional group of goats and the odd sprightly local who look like they are just popping out to the shops. At one point we were overtaken by an elderly lottery seller with strings of tickets around his neck. He stopped ahead of us to sell one of these to someone coming the other way, then raced off again, just as nimbly as if he had been nipping from bar to bar in Madrid.

We could see the path snaking up and away into the hazy distance, like an illustration straight from the pages of Grimms' fairy tales. In places it would momentarily divide, giving you a choice: a dark tunnel burrowed into the rock one way, a narrow, blind bend the other, each possibility equally as unclear and alarming. I half expected a troll to appear and tell us that going left would save us, whilst right would lead to certain death, and, like in the children's puzzles, you had three questions to discover whether or not he was a liar.

Having arrived at the end of the gorge, we stopped for a bean stew lunch at the hamlet of Poncebos, then set about the task of reaching Bulnes, a further three hour walk uphill. At that time, the only way in or out of Bulnes was on foot, and it was said to be the only remaining village in Europe that couldn't be reached by road, river or rail. Now there is a funicular railway, rumoured to be so ill prepared in case of fire that you are still better off going on foot.

We reached Bulnes late that afternoon. It was a minimalist masterpiece, a collection of earthy buildings, barns and muddy paths tucked into the folds of a fertile valley. Hand cut hay-pastures lay in judgment above it and silent scree slopes led on up from these to monosyllabic peaks. We booked into the *auberge*, then Jono went off to scale new heights whilst I followed the village stream, thick with reeds and inquisitive donkeys, to a heavenly meadow where I sat up to my neck in wild flowers, and pondered my options again.

Reconvening later in Bulnes' only bar, Jono and I congratulated ourselves on having got this far without incident, deciding we were fully prepared for the Pyrenees. We ordered a bottle of Asturian cider, and began talking to an Englishman who had come in and flung his back pack down on the floor. He, like the 'new' us, was also a keen walker, so we asked him if he had done any trekking in the Pyrenees.

'No,' he answered, 'I've always had a love affair with Spain you see.'

But evidently not with its geography.

≈

Three days later we were back in Madrid, proud of our mountaineering skills and, once again, barely able to walk. We had an appointment with Pablo at 11 o'clock the next morning to hang our pictures for the opening night. To confirm Jono's suspicions about Spanish punctuality, Pablo arrived half an hour late with a terrible hangover, and took us to another bar around the corner for a slow recuperative coffee. When finally we returned to the Cafe Belen it took close to three more hours to hang the prints. Pablo would put one on the wall, hang another next to it, then stand back and strike a contemplative pose.

'I don't know, I'm not sure,' he'd mutter, before asking our opinion, then trying both pictures somewhere else. On this went until, with all of us driven close to distraction, the perfect arrangement was discovered. When Pablo was finished, Jono and I went off to buy a gas stove and some back-up maps. Tomorrow we would head for the Pyrenees to start out eighteen day trek.

The exhibition clearly marked the end of that first period in Madrid. Whilst only a third of the way into the three accidental years that I have lived here, it looks more like a half-way point. Life changed dramatically in this first half, it was simply a matter of living out the repercussions after that. Besides, it would have been impossible, perhaps even detrimental to the health, to maintain the rhythm of those first nine months.

Summer had flooded the city, every surface of every street felt as if it had just been ironed, the heat smarting as The *Extranjeros* Out of Focus walked into the Fino Bar, for a preliminary bottle of *Fino*. A good evening was always guaranteed when started like that. The bottle finished, we changed to a bar next to the Cafe Belen, the zinc top, TV and rubbish all over the floor kind, and drank whiskey and coke. Nerves sufficiently calmed we made our grand entry to the exhibition and found that every single person that we had invited had turned up. It was packed. My Monday and Wednesday afternoon students were there, the Lopez sisters, Eva included, sat at a corner table with a few of the Friday evening group. Marina arrived with some of her friends. Many of the academy staff were meticulously making their way through the bottles of free wine.

We, the photographers, swanned around, 'famous' again, modestly accepting praise for our work, though not one of us sold a print. Pablo, having complemented us on the exhibition, and himself again on the judicious hanging of the pictures, sat at the end of his bar and looked on bemused, as surprised as we were that it was so full up.

Then Eva asked me the question that I had been hoping to avoid.

'Is she your girlfriend?' She pointed at Marina.

'Yes,' I said.

I'll never know what my answer meant to her, but I had this funny feeling then that just maybe, conceivably, she had been interested somewhere along the line. I haven't seen her since. I never phoned her again. It didn't seem right to continue *intercambio*-ing under the circumstances, and anyway, I was still telling her, just as I told everyone else, that I was definitely leaving Madrid.

There was a radiant atmosphere in the Belen that night, a convivial glow inflamed by the struggle against the heat and the soporific effects of the wine. Around two in the morning Jono, Marina and I left in a taxi. Jono may have had one Rioja too many, and had turned apple-white.

How the hell was I going to leave Madrid now? What on earth was I to do about my lack of flat and lack of job? I knew I was stuck again, that the options meant nothing, that again the sea would have to wait. But beyond that nothing was clear, nothing but the presence of Marina, friends in the city and a mad passion for Spain, in which the capital was so conveniently placed in the centre.

Off to the Pyrenees I thought, and think about it when you get back.

≈

Jono and I stood on, or rather clung to, a 45-degree scree slope, sweating hard, and swearing.

'Shit. Is this the right way?' I said.

'I think so, the map said to head straight up the middle,' said Jono.

'I don't feel particularly safe. At all.'

'We must be nearly at the top.'

'I'm not happy. Really not happy about this.'

We had just completed a three hour walk up a steep, dusty ski-run near Formigal that the book had down as a mild ascent, and this was the last straw. My rucksack felt like lead. This was good. It might pin me down and stop me falling off the mountain. To my right there was a patch of snow. We were somewhere above two thousand metres. One slip would mean tumbling down forty feet of loose gravel and rock to where the grass had stopped. There would definitely be cuts and blood. This was not fun.

When at last we reached the ridge at the top we consulted the map again. We had been following the red line that marked out the GR11 to the millimetre. Only now did we see the road on our left that zig-zagged easily up to our present position, carefully avoiding the scree. At least the view was magnificent. Far behind us, beyond the vast glacial valley whose side we had just ascended, lay a circle of saw-tooth peaks, draped in cloud, set against a thousand-mile sky. In front of us stretched another valley, big enough to hold an ocean, enclosed on both sides by high ridges which thrust up in places into single grey summits. We were balanced precariously in the middle, holding on for dear life, straddling a knife edge.

Our route down into this valley took all afternoon. Vultures and eagles passed high above, static patrols covering miles whilst hardly moving. We saw an Ibex, a glimpse of a fox, and a dead horse that had broken its leg and never been found. This was a place at the end of the world, existing in absolute silence, and I was happy at last to be there - providing I didn't break my leg. Near the bottom we passed a group of young Spaniards coming the other way, planning to spend a night in the valley, the first people we had seen all day. Then, as we descended an inhospitable path of pine trees and sharp granite boulders, we met a single file of several hundred sheep, trailed at the end by a grizzled old shepherd with torn clothes, broken shoes, and a dog.

'Have you seen any other sheep up there?' he asked.

'No, sorry.'

'Oh. Are you thirsty?'

'Yes,' we replied, and he led us back down the path for a few minutes to show us a brackish freshwater spring, before wishing us good luck and turning to catch up with his flock.

The book had promised a six hour day, nothing vigorous. We arrived at our campsite ten hours after we had set out, legs deeply unhappy. The next day was worse. Another 'light six hour day, ending in a mild descent' at first took us through open pastures and beautiful beech woods, home to invisible Iberian bears. But just before lunch, in a desolate high pass littered with vast deposits of rock, we lost the path, then momentarily lost each other. That, I thought, was that. Exhaustion had me already. I pictured a lamentable demise, the inevitable show-down with the vultures. I took out my compass and held on to it for dear life. Convinced that it would save me, I started plotting courses to random rocks, hoping to stumble across the path. Two minutes later Jono appeared from behind an enormous boulder, and we continued on our way. Hours later, at the end of a dismal and eternal forestry path, we got to the campsite marked in our guide. It was shut. Had been for over a year. Someone from the bar next door gave us a lift down the road to the nearest town. (What if there hadn't *been* a bar next door?) It had been another ten hour day. The following morning we took a six hour short-cut by road, narrowly escaping heat stroke and a running attack from a savage, rabid looking guard dog.

Enough was enough. Ten months in Spain had taken its toll. The fiestas, the bars, the teaching, the travelling, the *intercambios*, the exhibitions, the non-stop hand-clapping Sevillanas-dancing irrepressible excitement of an unsurpassable quality and quantity of life had finally worn me out. I awoke at five o'clock the next morning to take a series of buses back to Madrid.

The following evening I was back in the mountains again, with the car. Whilst I was gone Jono had done one more day with the book, walking to another campsite a little further along the route. When I arrived I found him huddled up in our tent, scratched all over and as white as a sheet.

'The book did say that it was challenging,' he said, 'but I got lost again. It was pouring with rain. I ended up in a valley that wasn't on the map, running along a stream full of brambles, surrounded by tall pine trees. I felt as if I was watching myself from above, like in a film. It was absolutely terrifying.'

A week later, with the GR11 book confined to the bottom of a rucksack and the rucksacks long since confined to the boot of the car, we drove into San Sebastian, after a series of 'easy and pleasurable descents'.

6th July 2001

I'm lying on the red double camping lilo in the pool, squinting through my sunglasses at the trees, listening to the wind in their branches, a deep exhale that sounds very much like the sea. The pool is pure Hockney. Rectangular, simple concrete borders, for the moment a perfect blue, a couple of plastic sun loungers cast onto flagstones beside it, a splash of strong colour from another, pink lilo. The house could be Hockney too, a single storey of even whitewashed shapes built into a split level plot of land. There is a large open terrace in front of the house, built over the garage on the lower level, and reached by stone steps guarded on one side by a giant green and yellow striped cactus that curls in and out of the undergrowth like a family of Boa Constrictors. Pines mark the boundaries of the dusty, sun-dried garden, casting shadows here and there, the trees a constant source of annoyance to Marina's father who is tired of unblocking needles from the little cleaning robot that sucks its way around the bottom of the pool. He is sitting up on the terrace above the garage in the shade, in sandals and swimming shorts, flicking silently through a Sunday supplement. Her mother wanders down to the pool and dips a toe into the water.

'Ay, it's freezing,' she says, 'I'm not swimming today.' Then she fetches a watering can and waters the plants in the oblong tubs around the pool before calling Marina up to the house to help prepare some salads.

Up here in the hills outside Madrid it's a little cooler, never much above thirty two degrees, but still I have to kick around a bit to manoeuvre the lilo into the corner of the pool where the trees provide a little shade, where the light that reaches my eyes comes split into thousands of pieces by the stirring branches above. And I wonder to myself if this isn't the very essence of the dream, a state of 'alegría', of happiness, content, the state of being in all that brightness, in all that light, in a land of cactus and crickets, softly afloat above cool blue water, listening to the trees.

Colmi, and Other Houses

My first trip up to the house in the hills, to 'Colmi', was not so idyllic. It was September again, when the summer pushes on through one last month, when a year feels like it might start afresh there and then. Back in Madrid after the Pyrenees, Marina had invited me up for a family lunch, a formal welcome. This would be a significant step. There are two types of boyfriend in Spain, those who know the parents and those who don't. Knowing the parents is tantamount to engagement, not knowing them means you'll either know them soon enough, or you won't be around for long. Had I been aware of these implications, I would have been dreading the encounter even more as we joined the masses pouring out of Madrid for Sunday lunch.

It's very common for the Madrileño who can afford it to have a second home in the Sierra just to the north of Madrid. Elevated above the plains, halfway between the city and the Guadarrama range's mountainous peaks, lie a string of villages whose cool clean air proves irresistible in summer. Families will uproot and relocate entirely in July and August, commuting daily down to work in the city, and coming out at weekends during the rest of the year to eat.

The whole family had gathered for the occasion, and a couple of relations had been thrown in for good measure. In all we numbered ten: parents, sister, brother, his long term girlfriend (who had long since met the parents), an aunt, an uncle, their daughter and Marina and I, all stretched out along a narrow table below a towering Eucalyptus tree. Spanish table talk began with a vengeance, oscillating wildly between a turn-taking strategy, whereby one person at a time holds forth loudly to the whole table, and what can best be described as 'total conversation', where each member of the assembled company will choose a partner, preferably on the opposite side of the table, and proceed to talk to, and at the same time as, them and everybody else. As each pair strives to be heard across and above the rest, the volume rises, voices battle for supremacy, and the table reaches a fever pitch. It's practically unbearable until, quite suddenly, just when I feel I'm about to explode into a scream of desperation, everyone shuts up and starts turn taking again.

Everyone that is, except me. Throughout the entire meal I was working so hard to understand what was being said, that by the time each subject had been processed they had moved on with lightning speed to the next. The whole experience was something akin to a two hour listening exam, conducted at a level way above my abilities. Failure now could mean complete humiliation. Without exception I would be asked for my views at the precise moment I had chosen momentarily to switch off and relax.

'What do you think Ben?' Marina's mother would ask, out of the blue. All eyes would now turn in my direction. I would madly examine her kind face and brown eyes for a clue towards the anticipated answer, then hazard a guess:

'*Si*? *Si*, *si*...' or 'well, maybe...,' by which time it didn't matter anyway as they were already talking about something else.

The main topic of conversation was food. I have since discovered this to be typical of all Spanish meal times. Great debates rage over which region is better for *jamon*, which restaurant for which fish, which bar for the juiciest *pincho* of *tortilla*. Favourite places and products are defended fiercely, as is the national cuisine. I have often tried convincing Spaniards to try Thai or Indonesian dishes. Impossible, it's all *Currrri*, a word rolled off the tongue with all the contempt normally held back for their worst nightmare of all, English food. French cuisine is similarly dismissed, with a single word that evidently leaves a bitter taste in the mouth: 'buttery'.

After lunch, my mind like putty, we adjourned to the pool to recline on towels and talk some more. All I could think of was escape with Marina, an after lunch walk to somewhere very far away. Then suddenly, at some imperceptible signal, everyone, Marina included, keeled over, closed their eyes, and went to sleep. The siesta.

This was a ploy for which I hadn't been prepared. Being British and thus unaccustomed to falling asleep every time I have lunch, I felt extremely put out. I couldn't go anywhere as I didn't know where I was, and was terrified of waking them all if I attempted to stand up and wander off. I felt that by being the only one still awake, I was under even greater scrutiny than before. Here I was, lounging in blissful silence beside a pool I daren't even get into, suffering my most awkward moment yet. Marina, I decided, was an absolute traitor for not having taken the opportunity to abscond with me in search of a moment's privacy. An hour or two passed with me frozen to the spot until, at another secret signal, everyone woke up, declared it was time for coffee and the advanced listening exam started afresh.

Mother: I want to get a new mobile phone...

Brother's girlfriend: I couldn't believe it when I got another wedding invitation...

Aunt: I'm sick of ironing...

Father: ... The food in Galicia is marvellous, particularly the...

Uncle: ... and baptisms, my God...

Sister: ... yes but the chicken is terrible...

Marina: ... where... tea towels... bills, I know

Mother: ...phone bills, in... what?

Sister: You don't know anything about driving too fast

Brother: ... churches... and the gazpacho was dread-...

Me (aside): *Ahhhhhhhhh!*

I felt ridiculous for not speaking, paranoid of being ignored, and utterly terrified of being spoken to. That evening I returned to Madrid a mental wreck, swearing naively that this was an experience which I would never be repeating again. Ever. A few weeks and several family meals later, I had given up, comforting my bewildered brain with a new mantra: 'at least it's good for my Spanish'.

Within a few months I was managing to answer queries with near certainty as to what I had actually been asked. Nowadays I can hold forth in short bursts to the table, though the periods of total conversation still destroy me, their intensity and impracticality destined one day, I'm convinced, to drive me insane.

≈

At this time I was sleeping on the sofa in what had, only 6 weeks before, been my flat. So much for leaving Madrid. I wasn't unhappy to be back, but I had nothing to do and nowhere to live. As soon as possible I would have to get a job and a flat. After a mild anti-teaching crisis, fretting about what else I could feasibly do, I had a couple of interviews along the lines of, 'Can you speak English? - You're hired,' and started giving classes again. This, however, was a million miles away from the serious academy work I had landed myself in the year before. Four evenings a week I would mope up to the north of the city and prostitute my language to bored professionals across a table piled high with spare computer parts. When they bothered to turn up the majority spoke in Spanish and ignored me.

David, a cheeky young man with a Quentin Tarantino leer, constantly questioned my ability to teach:

'I think you shouldn't explain things to us like that, it doesn't help us you know.'

'I'm sorry?' I said, (actually thinking - Who the hell do you think you are? Do you really think I enjoy ploughing all the way up here at six thirty at night to be told how to explain words like 'pastry' to idiots like you?)

'Yes, it doesn't help to us that you are explaining this in *Spaniss*, it would be better in *Engliss*, no?'

At first I grew to hate him, then almost to like him, until finally I contacted my agency, told them his level was too high for the group, and had him transferred on to someone else. No messing around at this level. I was no longer in it for the pedagogical prestige.

The rest of my hours I made up with various unreliable and geographically displaced private classes, all the mad running around the city just about compensated for by a four day week and the decent hourly rate.

If the teaching was bad, then the housing situation was disastrous. With the impending introduction of the Euro, a lot of *dinero negro*, 'black', undeclared and un-taxed money had to rapidly disappear back into the Spanish economy. The answer was for these invisible pesetas to be put into something solid before they disappeared for good. Everyone was building extensions onto their Sierra homes, doing up their flats, or simply buying up property as fast as possible. Flats that had always been sidelined for an easy rental income were now being put on the market by vendors confident of a quick and easy sale.

In this climate my chances of finding a nice one-bedroom flat to rent were slim from the outset. Having no official job, and therefore no *nomina*, or payslip, to wave at potential landlords sank me for good. The few flats that did appear in the local small-ads would be set upon by crowds of desperate house hunters who would queue up outside the building an hour before they had been told to arrive. My despair at discovering that half of Madrid had got their first was compounded further by the typically appalling state of the flat on offer: tiny, overpriced and in total disrepair. Then came the final insult, when it was given to the first *nomina*-ed Spaniard through the door.

It was depressingly clear that by simply wanting a place to live on my own I was asking too much. My only chance would be a personal recommendation from a friend, from Marina's family perhaps, to someone who would give me first look at a flat before it hit the papers. A chance came at last from Jackie, my fellow photographer.

'A friend of mine is off to Cuba for a month, he's got a lovely house up the Castellana and wants me to house sit. You can have my flat in the meantime.' I was off the sofa at last, into her compact bohemian flatlette, looking over a lively plaza in the 19th century quarter of Tribunal. A step in the right direction.

Next she spoke to her landlady about an ideal flat right next door to hers. It was being done up, would be ready by the end of the month, hadn't yet reached the public ear, and could really be mine, albeit for an exorbitant monthly fee. I already pictured myself at one of the *salon* balconies, wine in hand, hosting many an arty soiree, lording it over my own personal, diminutive Plaza Mayor.

≈

The travels continued. Marina and I were keen to capitalise on any opportunity for a weekend away. Her parents had grown up in an era when, under Franco's dictatorial regime, it had been illegal to kiss in the streets. The moral clock had ticked somewhat slowly since then and an unmarried girl living at home - as they all do - would not usually be allowed to stay the night with a boyfriend, no matter where he came from or what he believed in. Marina had a proper job, as an I.T. consultant, was financially independent and well into her twenties, yet none of this counted for anything. Rules were rules. Despite all this, going away for the weekend together was somehow completely acceptable - out of sight, out of mind perhaps.

In the months that led up to Christmas we visited deep green Cantabria, where hunters gathered with hounds in high windy passes, and Murcia, where we swam from golden deserted coves in the cool Mediterranean Sea. In the Sierra de Gredos, a hundred kilometres to the west of Madrid, we found a rich microclimate of thick rusty ferns, cacti, olives, and dewy terraced hills steeped in mist and the delectable, intoxicating aroma of wild thyme.

We went to Seville, the city's orange trees and chattering plazas still basking in a secret supply of warm sunlight. I particularly remember the journey there on the luxurious AVE high speed train, rushing across the dusty Meseta plains, past mesmerising patterns of infinite squat olive trees, molten hills erupting from a hundred thousand earthenware fields and low, fluffy cartoon clouds, their smooth bottoms casting smudgy black shadows onto the scene below.

The effect these landscapes had on me seemed profound, a widening of the eyes, the ecstasy described by Brenan repeated again and again, until it seemed that I had half a grasp on something intangible, some greater reality where everything was more beautiful than it ought to be, nothing religious, but internally enticing, impossible to keep hold of for long, and lost again the moment I headed reluctantly back into the busy streets of Madrid. I was addicted to Spain, to these travels that were affording me a glimpse of something I couldn't quite yet understand.

And as we ran around the country I was discovering something else, that the people were just as fascinating as the countryside, and curiously, that some of them didn't actually consider themselves to be Spanish at all. In October, travelling alone to Tarragona by train, I passed a familiar slogan scrawled on a station wall near Valencia: 'this town is not Spain'.

I was heading for the heart of Catalonia, not quite sure what to expect. A few Madrileños had told me that the Catalans were industrious but stingy and often plain rude. One of my students made it quite clear what she thought: 'they won't speak to any one from Madrid in Spanish, only Catalan, and they deliberately give us wrong directions.'

Not all accounts were quite so damning. In his marvellous 'Homage to Catalonia', George Orwell claimed to be 'struck by their decency; above all their straight-forwardness and generosity.' And a friend who lived in Barcelona spoke of a powerful Catalan optimism. 'If you watch the weather on Catalan TV,' she said, 'then on the Spanish national TV, the forecast is *always* better on the Catalan channel. Always!'

Tarragona is a working town and seaside resort some one hundred kilometres down the coast from Barcelona. At the station I was met by English friends and our Catalan connection, Monica. Born in Tarragona and now living in England, she had flown back for the biannual Concurs de Castells. This was what we had come to see: the human castles competition.

That evening at dinner in her family home, her father expressed his indignation at the event.

'Why would any parent make their child climb 12 metres into the air, knowing they would almost certainly fall down again? It's madness!'

He spoke to us in Spanish, but communication between family members was always in Catalan. The language is an odd mixture, part Castillian Spanish, part French, part its own. If you know something of the first two you may be able to read it, but 80 per cent of 'Spaniards' will claim that it's impossible to understand when spoken. Yet in Catalonia it thrives. In the regions of Galicia, Valencia and the Basque country, the situation is exactly the same, with regional dialects predominating in schools and many family homes. As language is so closely allied with identity in these areas, it is no wonder Spain often has a hard time just trying to be Spanish.

We ate *Fideos*, noodles cooked in fish broth then toasted in the oven, and *Zapatillas*, bread covered in cured ham, fresh garlic mayonnaise, and aubergine. After the meal her father brought out his bottles. A dozen liquors and spirits were thrust upon us in dizzying measures - Chartreuse from France, fiery clear Orujo from the North, later Cuban rum - it was Orwell's generosity, and not a bit of the stinginess I had heard about in Madrid.

At ten o'clock the next morning we walked into Tarragona's bullring. People had been queuing since eight to get a good seat behind their team, and we had trouble finding a space for the five of us amongst the twelve thousand other spectators. Below us on the bullring floor stood the eighteen teams, in tight groups of bright colours. There were fifty to a hundred people to each team, dazzling pools of reds, greens, and blues. Outside some twenty ambulances stood at the ready, while fifty Red Cross paramedics waited nervously in the wings, stretchers propped against the wall.

No sooner had we sat down, than the *Joves Xiquets de Valls* team announced it was about to perform a *Quatre de Nou*.

'Ooh! A four of nine,' said Monica, 'four people wide, nine storeys high, you're very lucky to see such a difficult one first.'

What followed was quite extraordinary. About forty team members stood in a tight circlular scrum, a *pinya*, heads down and arms stretched forwards towards the middle. Up onto this mass climbed four burly men who stood at the centre in a small square, locking rigidly together by reaching out and clasping each others shoulders. Then across the *pinya* and up onto their shoulders climbed four more men. With this lot standing locked into place the *castell* was now three storeys high, time to decide whether or not it was stable enough to go ahead.

Traditional pipe music burst into the arena, the signal to continue, and a wave of bodies shinned up the backs of those already in position. Storey four stood up and locked in, then five, a thin human spire now emerging from the tight circular base. The bottom began to wobble and the crowd fell silent. Up went storey six, then seven.

Now the crowd was breathless. Half way up the tower, poised to shoot to the summit, were two eight-year-old boys, the top two storeys always comprising just one tiny child a piece. The first scrambled up over the last bottoms and backs and bent across the storey below then, finally, the last child reached the top and, sitting on his friend, forty feet above ground, thrust one arm into the air. The castle was complete, the crowd euphoric, and in a flash the nine layers of castlers slid down each other like firemen down poles, before the lower storeys could take the strain no more.

These Herculean efforts carried on well into the afternoon, the most impressive feats of strength and agility I had ever seen, though not without incident. About three in five of the Castells went badly wrong. Usually it was the moment after the top child had raised his arm to claim the points that the whole thing came crashing down onto the *pinya* in a mass of flailing limbs. This is horrendous to watch. Only when the child is pulled from the melée unharmed does the crowd breath a sigh of relief. At least ten people were carted off in neck braces at our end, men, women and children alike. The paramedics stretchered them off and the ambulances came and went all day. One year a man had allegedly been paralysed from the waist down in a *castell* collapse. They say he now eats in all the town's restaurants for free.

The Castells began in the nineteenth century near Tarragona, competing happily until the 1930's when Franco came along. Once his right wing armies had crushed the Republicans, thus ending the civil war in 1939, Franco spent the next thirty years expunging Spain of all things regionalist, coming down particularly hard on the Basques and the Catalans. Local dialects and traditional fiestas like the Concurs de Castells were banned and driven firmly underground until his death in 1975. Then a democracy was established in Spain, outlying regions like Catalonia formed independent local governments, and everything Franco had prohibited rushed back into popular culture again.

Half way through the day, amid four of eights and five of nines, there was a sudden uproar from the crowd. Participants and spectators alike were pointing at one of the bullring's upper balconies. Three policemen were talking to someone above one of the bright red and yellow Catalan flags that were draped at intervals around the ring.

'Everyone thinks they're trying to remove the flag,' said Monica.

The crowd was appalled, shouting and swearing until the police eventually disappeared from sight and a victorious chant of 'Catalonia - Catalonia' sailed forth.

'If you brought out the Spanish flag now,' shouted Monica above the noise, 'it would probably be burnt. It's stupid. After Franco there was an over-reaction, like a backlash towards everything Catalan, but this sort of thing goes too far.'

Soon afterwards there was more excitement as the *La colla dels Xiquets de Vals* team announced it would try for a three of ten. This had only ever been accomplished twice before, and never in competition. Worth thirteen thousand two hundred and twenty points it would secure them first prize. A huge *pinya* formed, then another group jumped up to form another, smaller *pinya* on top. Then again a third *pinya* went up, and it started to look like a giant wedding cake. Three enormous men got up onto this lot and locked into place. From now on the *castell* would continue up in groups of three until the the two tiny children completed the last two storeys. Was this the celebrated Catalan optimism?

Yes. The music started, everyone drew breath and the last castlers raced up into place. Finally, there it was, three pinyas, five storeys of three, then the penultimate child, and at last, with the whole thing wobbling excruciatingly, a tiny child at the top, his arm thrust into the air. The bullring exploded into delirious applause as the whole lot came crashing down to earth. I can only imagine how it must feel for an eight year old: to be perched fifty feet in the air, to crown a historic castle and win the competition for your team in front of twelve thousand people, and finally the horrific fall to the ground.

When the excitement had died down, there was an announcement by the judges. The town council would like to make it very clear that at no point had there been any intention to remove or in anyway tamper with the Catalan flag. The police had simply been responding to complaints that objects had been thrown from an upper balcony. More cheering from the crowd. Behind us, tied to a wooden balustrade, I noticed a solitary *Ikurriña,* the union-jack-like Basque national flag, a further reminder that Spain is but a collection of proud, diverse and irrepressible nations, the many different 'Spains' that I had previously imagined were one.

≈

The flat next door to Jackie's was temporarily put on hold. The landlady had an obligation to a niece, and in Spain, where loyalty to the family is all, a word-of-mouth promise to an unknown Englishman is guiltlessly undone. Still, she thought I could probably have it in a few weeks when the niece moved on. Back to square one, and with Jackie in need of her flat again, I set out on a series of unhappy flat hops. I spent a week opposite Marina's parents in a flat they were waiting to lease (far too expensive for me to take on, and a little too close for comfort). Then I moved into a friend of the family's spare room, normally sidelined for foreign students of Spanish in need of a cosy homely environment, something I definitely didn't need.

The place was tucked up on the sixth floor of a mid-century apartment block, in a residential area to the west of the city centre. The widowed mother was kind, as was her son. He was about my age, still living at home of course, and liked to sing me Eric Clapton ballads to the accompaniment of his guitar after lunch. I didn't feel even close to finding the privacy I so deeply desired from my future one-bedroom flat.

Plus there was one other tenant, a strange looking lady from South America, studying science, biology I think, for an MA. She sat next to me on the sofa when I arrived and introduced herself.

'I'm from PARAGUAY, PA - RA - GUAY. It's a country, in SOUTH AMERICA, SOU - TH A -...' She had an infuriating habit of appearing at my meal times, and furtively examining what I was cooking. She would accost me as I was walking home from the Metro, lost in a book. She would knock on my door to deliver telephone messages that I had already seen pinned to the kitchen wall, grinning at me as if I were a rare museum exhibit ('Englishman, circa 1972'), and enunciating her Spanish as if she were trying to educate a parrot. This could not go on. I promised myself that it would only be for a fortnight.

The landlady's infamous niece, however, showed no sign of budging from the flat next to Jackie. Christmas arrived and I had been confined to the foreign-student-bedsit for close to six weeks. Then - how could I have failed to see it coming - it transpired that the niece had become a little more settled than she had previously imagined, and wouldn't be moving after all. There would be no arty soirees, no drinks on the balcony above the plaza. I left for Christmas in England, telling my homely Spanish family that I had got the other flat anyway, and, sadly, wouldn't be returning to them when I got back.

That's when I decided. Somewhere between the holly and the ivy, Christmas day and New Year's Eve, I realised what it was that had to be done. I saw that if I were ever to galvanise these wanderings into something productive, if I were ever to get on with anything, then I would have to look for a flat to buy in Madrid.

8th July 2001

I'm driving down the hill in the dark, the back way out of El Escorial. Marina and I spent the whole afternoon at Colmi again, me on the lilo, her on a towel in the shade, drifting in and out of sleep. Then we drove up here for supper on the terrace at 'Charoles'. The waiter gave us both a straw hat on the way out.

Driving out this way you see the town's monastery, Filipe II's dream realised, a building so enormous that seen close up each section would in itself be an immense building in its own right. Seen from afar, floodlit at night, it dominates the darkness so masterfully that somehow I wish it were even bigger, the biggest, most ridiculously huge building on earth. We circle down towards the main road that leads back towards Madrid, passing the field at the bottom where they say that the Virgin appeared. A few cars are parked up in the lay-by, and glancing through the iron gates that open onto the fields I see wide magical circles, sparkling candles placed by the faithful, like silent, over-sized Catherine wheels, stuck fast beneath the twisted oak trees. I'm not sure she'll be back tonight my friends, I think, and we are gone.

It's very late by the time we get back to Madrid. There has been another power cut, this time in the plaza at the bottom of our street. I drive through after dropping Marina off, looking for somewhere to park. The plaza is seething and devious in the dark. Some groups have a guitar, everyone a litre bottle of Mahou beer. Spaniards mingle with Morrocans, Dominicans, Indians, Bangalis, people from the Middle East and Eastern Europe, probably even some English and French. No longer are the Chinese alone in Madrid, not in the Plaza de Lavapies at least. A lot has changed in three years; Spain's attraction grows ever more far reaching.

Last night two Morrocans were caught a hundred meters from the Spanish coast on a pedalo, an old, iron craft, buoyed up by long rusty floats. They had hired it from a beach in Tangiers at seven o'clock the previous evening, pointed for Spain, and pedalled for twelve hours without stopping. Within sight of land, of Europe, they met a strong current and, too exhausted to reach shore, were spotted at daylight and picked up. Soon the Guardia Civil will deport them. Over one thousand Africans made the break for Spain that night. The fifteen kilometres of water that separate Africa from us were calm, tempting. Most were caught. Every year thousands more don't even get the chance to be deported, churned up instead in the lethal straits of Gibraltar, then washed up on the beach at Bolonia and emitted, sandy and twisted, on national television.

I park the car in Atocha, and walk home. Thank God we're going to the north coast this week. We have seven days to cool off in Asturias, away from the searing streets and the chattering masses, to get out of all this for a while.

In the flat I fling open the balcony doors, letting in the heat and the lifeless leaves of the trees. The air is solid, cloying, there isn't even a hint of a breeze. I sit down and look at this text, irritated by the heat, by an argument in the street below. I must get this done before my Spanish summer comes to a sweltering end, before I leave in a few weeks for a month in England, mostly though before September arrives. I will have been here three years by then and I feel a great circle swooping round to a close, that from it another will emerge, and that this is an old project that I have to complete before whatever's coming next can take its turn.

A trip to the *Notario*

The search for a flat started as soon as I got back to Madrid after Christmas. I moved into the hostel where I had spent my first days in the city, little more than sixteen months before, determined to stay there as long as it took.

The *barrio* of Lavapies seemed like a good area in which to concentrate my efforts. It was central, familiar, lively, and architecturally old enough to be possessed of a certain charm. Just outside Madrid de Los Austrias, the mediaeval quarter, the apartment buildings of Lavapies began to spring up in the 1820's, probably replacing an area of slums, fouled streams and vegetable patches.

Buying a property here would almost certainly be a good investment. Prices were comparatively low as the average misinformed Madrileño still thought the area to be run-down, too old and unsafe at night. Not so. In fact it had been earmarked by the European Community for substantial regenerative funding and was already decidedly smarter than it had been two or three years before. As for the issue of safety at night, with so much life in the streets everyone lived under the scrutiny of a permanent neighbourhood watch. Finally, occupying such a central position in a European capital meant (touch wood) that prices would always go up. Here, I thought, was another Clapham or Brixton: sooner or later there would be roller-coaster regeneration, then all the lawyers and media-*riche* would move in.

Thus, with the small ad's paper once again to hand, my search began. Estate agents have a hard time of it in Spain. The canny house seller will cut them out of the equation and reap extra profit by selling his property direct. When you see how well everyone bypasses the estate agent here, it makes you wander why they exist at all, anywhere.

Things got off to a bad start. Nine out of ten places were gone before they came out in print, already sold via a family tie, or a friend of a friend. I feared that once again the Englishman with a limited network of contacts would need a lot of luck.

Somewhere came up on the Calle del Fé. Third floor, windows onto the street, a good size. Marina and I went round early one

Saturday morning. We were received by a short, dumpy man with a smear of stubble on his chin and a pair of slippers on his feet. The living room windows looked straight across the narrow street to a grey concrete facade and despite the owners insistence that 'the sun comes round in the afternoon', it was obvious that the flat would receive little light. He had removed whatever original features there might once have been, tiled the floors from bathroom to bedroom in glossy white, and sprayed the walls with the characteristic, bubbly white paint that Spaniards have a passion for and called *Gotelet* - the aesthetic equivalent of wood-chip wallpaper. No good.

Another hopeful place came up in the Calle Tribulete, hopeful in that it was in Lavapies and hadn't been sold yet. I trudged up the tight noisy street to see it with Marina's mother, whose knowledge of the second-hand flat market we all held in high regard. She was a connoisseur of the property pages, having already moved a few small flats on and off the market herself.

'What do you think?' she said.

'Well, I'm not sure about the floors,' the glossy tiles again, 'and I don't really like the doors,' frosted picture-glass in imitation wood, 'and I'm not too keen on the *Gotelet*.'

'It's very practical you know.'

Marina's Mother had a quick haggle over the price anyway, to make something of the trip, and we left, both unimpressed.

It was already obvious that I was embroiled in a battle of the tastes, a race against time, to find a place before it was gutted of all charm and antiquity, before it was modernised beyond repair in readiness for the marketplace.

The third place to come up, towards the end of January, was on the Calle Lavapies. It was almost too expensive, but big for the price at seventy eight metres squared. Marina's mother and I stood on the pavement outside, considering the crumbling facade while we waited for Pilar, our contact, to appear. A bar on the ground floor, Casa Juanito, as zinc and filth as they come, was full of bored looking old men in carpet slippers. On the other side of the front door was a Chinese restaurant where no-one seemed to be doing any work.

A weasely old man with a deep frown and flat feet appeared, leaned on his stick and sighed.

'Do you live in this building?' Marina's mother asked.

'Yes,' he replied, in a strangled, acidic voice.

'Is it in good condition inside?'

'Oh yes, marvellous.'

'Thank you,' she said and, 'seemed like a nice man,' once he had waddled off again.

Twenty minutes after the appointed time a blonde bombshell swept down the road in a white Golf gti, shouting from the window that she was just looking for somewhere to park. Ten minutes later she reappeared, clicking up the street in her heels, unscrumpling her skirt and straightening her hair. Middle-aged, smoker's rasp, dashing, polite, the stuff soap operas are made of, Pilar was a friend of the family who owned the flat.

'So sorry I'm late,' she beamed, and we forgave her at once as kisses flew from cheek to cheek.

She let us into the building, apologising again, this time for the rusting letter boxes and bulging walls in the hall. As we climbed the wide timber staircase I ran my hand over the original wooden handrail and averted my eyes from the finger width cracks in the supporting walls. We stopped on the third floor, Pilar fumbled for some keys, led us to an alcove concealing two deep brown doors, considered briefly which was ours and let us in.

A dark corridor led round to the right to a pair of doors and another straight passage way. We opened the door on the right and walked into a largish room with windows in one corner that opened onto a wide interior light shaft, or *patio*. We prized open the windows. It looked like all the glass was on the verge of falling out. A strong stench of oil and sardines rose from the bar's kitchen below. Pilar found the fuse box and there was light. Original floor tiles appeared, symmetrical curving patterns in burnt crimson and dark olive, filthy but there. Dubious, green leafy paper adorned the walls, lightened in rectangular patches from top to bottom where pictures had hung before.

We went through the next door, to the kitchen. Windows again onto the same *patio*, an early twentieth-century coal-fired cooking range and an enormous oblong enamelled stone sink. All the right alarm bells were ringing. In the corner behind another door was the lavatory. We started down the long corridor pursued by Pilar.

'You can see it's got tremendous potential, you can get rid of these dreadful floor tiles and that terrible kitchen sink...' she said, all the time a slight air of panic in her voice, as if at any moment we might say, 'Who are you trying to kid?' and march out of the front door.

Symmetrical slim rooms just past the kitchen held a defunct fifties washing machine, a stinking fridge, and a beautiful, tapless and antiquated enamel washbasin, a plastic jug at its feet.

'Ahhhh, yes...' said Pilar, apologising again, 'you would need to put in a bathroom. They only had this for washing before.'

My god, I thought, until the end of the twentieth century they washed from a sink with no running water. At least there was a loo, one or two houses in the area still shared one external, corridor lavatory per floor.

At the end of the passageway stood two awkward-sized rooms that overlooked the street, one not quite big enough, the other too small, the two separated by a flimsy partition wall.

Pilar gave it a thump: 'Tear this down straight away and you'll have a lovely *salon.*' In each room an overindulgent, kitch chandelier hung at head height from drooping ceilings, above more elegantly patterned *terrazzo* floors.

We opened the shutters and the balcony doors, letting in the trees, leafless and wintry, but nevertheless tall, embracing trees. As they grew just to the left and the right of the flat, light poured in from the ample space left in front. Opposite was a freshly painted, late nineteenth-century apartment building, a vision of what this block might also one day become.

Behind each of these rooms were two more, small and windowless, enough room for a double bed and little else, and currently full of outsized wardrobes, ornate, chrome bedsteads, and rolled mattresses of undiscernible odour and age.

'There we are,' sighed Pilar, 'a lot of space, really a beautiful flat.... all this furniture would stay of course... what do you think?'

Clearly she couldn't keep this up for much longer, the forced smile was beginning to crack at the seams.

The place hadn't been touched, hadn't been Spanish-ified yet. Why not?

'Who lived here before?' said Marina's mother.

'An old lady.' The house, she explained, was an inheritance, split between three children who wanted a quick sale, no hassle, no desire to plough money into it first. I imagined the old mattresses and bedsteads being stacked away soon after their mother was carried, for the last time, out of the front door.

I wandered through to the kitchen again and stared at that magnificent sink. This wouldn't last long in the hands of a forewardthinking Spaniard. I went back into the little room with the basin. How had that poor woman washed herself in winter, with no central heating?

'What about the state of the building, are there plans to do it up at all?' said Marina's mother.

'Ah!' Pilar leapt into action again, 'the neighbours are all agreed on a plan of reforms, to be implemented very soon, it's all signed and sealed, the first thing they'll do is stick in a lift. Imagine, no more need to climb the stairs!' Marina's mum seemed particularly pleased by this. No-one would buy beyond the third floor in a building without a lift, and even being on the third floor was pushing things. A lift, a restored building inside and out, plus a major overhaul of the flat itself - even with the extra spending these would require the price they were asking guaranteed a good investment in the end.

'Of course if we were interested the price would have to come down,' said Marina's mum, warming up for battle, 'look at all the work that needs doing: masonry, plumbing, heating, painting...' I took a last look out onto the street and shut the heavy interior shutters.

Shutting out the trees. That's what had got me, the presence of life at the window. That hint of country, the potential for green. More than the sinks, the old tiled floors, the shutters, the lack of *Gotelet* paint, or the simple miracle of having got there first. Above all these essential elements of my romantic preconception of flat-owning abroad, what did it was the added delight of living in the tops of the trees.

We said we would phone. Pilar disappeared in a flurry of jacket straightening, kisses to cheeks, evident relief, and waves. From then on, from the moment I decided that it had to be that flat, that the chances of finding another in such original condition were nigh-on impossible, everything was taken out of my hands.

Marina's mum started furious telephone negotiations, Spanish style, enough to send any Anglo-Saxon to an early, stress-related grave. They wanted 17.5 million pesetas, clearly too much, but perhaps a third of the price of a similarly located central London flat of the same size.

'Why not offer 15.5?' I said. Marina's mum phoned through an offer of 14. Pilar thought it unlikely that the family would be interested. She would be in touch. I despaired. They would laugh our offer out of the running and accept someone else's. Days passed. Agonising. Nothing happened. I begged Marina to ask her mother to phone again. She did. The family were still thinking about it. The next day they phoned back with 16.5.

'Leave them a day or two,' said Marina's mum, 'then I'll offer them 14.5.' I pleaded the case for offering 15.5 immediately, but to no avail. Eventually my next offer was put in, as a compromise, at 15. Once again Pilar didn't think they would be terribly interested, but she would let us know. Two days passed. No one seemed in the least bit worried but me.

Pilar phoned back with a final deal of 15.5. Marina's mum still wanted to go for 15.

'No! Take it!' I said, and at last, two or three days later, Pilar phoned back with a date for the sale. Marina's mother had saved me two million pesetas, enough for most of the work on the flat. I was grateful, shattered, and amazed.

In the two weeks before the sale I imagined a survey of the flat would be required. The expertise of Marina's father, an architect, was, however, all it seemed I would need:

'I don't really think we do surveys here,' said Marina, 'but dad will have a look and we'll talk to the neighbours, that'll be fine.'

Her father was worried about a few drooping ceilings and bowed floors. At some point in the future the ceilings would need opening up throughout the whole building, so that the old wooden beams could be strengthened with new, steel joists. He wouldn't say don't buy it, or do, but pointed out the risk of taking on somewhere which might need an unspecified amount of money ploughing into it in the future. Wise words. Perhaps he was saying don't buy it after all.

What neighbours we could find spoke assuredly of the future rehabilitation of the building, and thought that indeed they had heard something about a lift being put in. We tracked down another architect at the local council, in charge of all European funded building work in the area.

'That is a place with many problems,' she said, '*muchisimos problemas*,' but when pressed admitted that she didn't think it would actually fall down. I fretted. It was just what I wanted in practical and aesthetic terms, but a financial hazard, and in desperate need of the promised repairs. There was still time to back out. Marina liked the flat, recognised all the problems, and patiently bore the brunt of my last minute indecisions.

'What about the cracks in the stairs?' I would ask her.

'It's an old building, come on, what do you expect?'

'What about your father? What do you think he thinks I ought to do?'

'I don't know, he's not going to tell you whether to buy it or not.'

'And the council woman?'

'I don't know.'

'Well what do you think, should I buy it or not?'

'*Ay* Ben, please, you are the only one who can decide!'

≈

On the day of the sale Marina's father had agreed to provide moral and lingual support. We had arranged to meet outside the *Notario*'s office at half past twelve, a *Notario* being the appropriate type of solicitor to oversee this sort of thing. There we were to meet Pilar and the hitherto unseen sellers, the Calvete Muñoz family.

It was February 14th, Valentines day. The weather was bitter and I had a terrible cold. I was still extremely nervous, feeling like my life had long since spiralled out of control. This would not be a step I could readily undo. In half an hour I would no longer be able to up sticks and leave the country, or for that matter the city, on a moment's whim. Shouldn't all this be happening to me in England, I thought, where perhaps I would know what I was really doing?

Marina's father was nowhere to be seen. At twelve I gave up and went on in. A receptionist showed me down a grubby corridor leading to offices packed floor to ceiling with files, then waved me into a small, crowded room. The Calvete Muñoz family rose to greet me. Pilar, who had been concealed behind the door, leapt up, immaculate, and radiantly blonde. She introduced me to her charges, sealed the introduction with a round of kisses, mumbled something about previous arrangements and disappeared. I felt like a fugitive who had just fallen headlong into the trap, or a rare species handed proudly over to the zoo. Left alone with this edgy group of strangers, I felt my foreignness like a great sign around my neck, alight with buzzers and bells, asking in bold capital letters, 'What right does this Englishman imagine he has to be here buying your house from you?'

With barely a look at my captors, I sat down. A junior solicitor hidden behind a large monitor began to read through what I guessed were the contracts of sale. Flushed with congestion and nerves, I became Spanish-deaf and couldn't understand a thing. Like the convicted man in the dock, I spoke only when asked to confirm my name. Where was Marina's dad? Where oh where oh where was he? The numbers were against me. Without his help I could never expect a fair trial.

Preliminary proceedings completed - whatever they were - we were guided back to reception, there to await the final, damning audience with the *Notario*. Now, with time on our hands, my opponents and I could size each other up. There were the three siblings, the inheritees. Valentin (appropriately named, given the date), was retired, a sprightly man in grey suit and tie, whose small features squashed up around a thin moustache. Next to him was Augustine, a younger, well built and wary looking man, who had me constantly pinned down in the corner of one eye. And then the sister, quiet, neat and kind-faced. She might have been a nun had it not been for the husband in tow, a swanky, arrogant man who was some other kind of lawyer, a stand-in legal man that they had brought along in case things got nasty. Valentin got up occasionally and paced about, covering the exits, while Augustine rocked his shoulders like a boxer squaring up for a fight. Neither the sister, or her husband, would look me in the eye.

At last, with my nerves at breaking point, just as we had been assembled by a receptionist and told that the *Notario* was ready, my star witness arrived. Marina's father strolled in, apologised for the delay, politely greeted the enemy, and casually asked me if everything was going O.K. In we went.

We took sides across a large oval polished-oak table. Manicured legal volumes lined the walls. Whilst we waited for the *Notario* to come in Valentin told us about his walks:

'I do fifteen kilometres every day you know, without fail,' he said, either to lighten things up a little or let us know that he really was a pretty serious kind of a guy.

The Notario appeared through a grand old door at the other end of the room. Grey haired, with steel spectacles, he was part headmaster, part judge. I half expected him to reach into a leather box and bring out a curled legal wig, and half to wack a cane down on the table and send me out of the room. The secretary appeared with a pile of papers which he checked through then read aloud to us in an eternal mumble of more unintelligible Spanish.

'Are you happy?' The Notario had stopped and was addressing me. No, but it hardly seemed appropriate that I should say so. All eyes in the room were upon me. The Calvete Muñoz clan looked ready to leap to their feet if I made a bid for escape. In their eyes I was probably the only man in Madrid crazy enough to buy a flat in that condition, and at any moment they thought I might click, and flee. The stakes were high, this was their inheritance on the line. I turned to Marina's father.

'Am I happy?'

'Yes,' he said, 'everything seems to be fine.'

Papers were distributed and the Notario passed me his gold-leaf fountain pen. I thought a bible might appear, over which we would all raise our hands and swear an oath. One by one we signed, in triplicate. I passed each sibling their bank cheque for a third of the 15.5. The *Notario* asked us to stand while he delivered the verdict, handing down my sentence:

'Congratulations,' he said, 'you are now the owner of a flat in Lavapies.'

Valentine stretched across the table and shook my hand with his powerful fifteen-kilometres-a-day grip. Augustin dropped his shoulders and gave me a 'you better be more careful next time' glare. The sister offered a conciliatory smile, as her legal husband slipped quietly out of the door.

That night Marina and I sat on the dusty floor of the larger room at the front. I felt as if I were recovering from a painful trip to the dentist, though in this case it had not been for an extraction, but a significant and agonising addition. We had arranged a pair of candles on the floor, the green patterned wallpaper shivered in their cool, silver light. A dog's bark sprang up from the street. We ate blanched asparagus from a tin and swigged Cava from a bottle.

'Happy Valentines day!' she said, 'you've got a lot of work ahead...'

17th July 2001

I'm walking up the street towards the front door, leaden legged, pushing my way through the dense afternoon heat, and... what the hell is he doing? Oh God I hope it isn't a rat, I can cope with anything but rats...

Through the glass in the front door I can see the weasely old man with the strangled voice, half stooped, using his stick to bash something on the floor. The something seems to be trying to escape, and the blows are raining left right and centre. Then I see a couple of feathers fly into the air. Oh God, it's a pigeon. I turn on the spot, walk ten paces back down the hill, and stop. Looking back up towards the building I see the door open and a grey/white/red ball of fluff fly onto the pavement, closely followed by weasle-man's foot. Out he comes, waving his stick and bang! he boots it another ten feet into the middle of the road, where it lies quivering.

I rush past him, dive through the front door and run up the stairs to my flat. There is a smell of stew. Someone is shouting and someone else has their TV on far, far too loud. An old woman in dressing gown and slippers peers out of her darkened room to watch me unlock the door. Inside, I rush to the windows and look down at the road. The pigeon is gone! Who took it?

It's so hot, so drainingly hot, and all I want to do is write more of this, but I'm exhausted, and disturbed by the thing with the pigeon. I lie down on the bed, and drift in and out of dreamy summer sleep.

Marina comes back and I tell her about the pigeon.

'Do you think the Chinese restaurant took it?' I say.

'No, the old guy probably, I expect he killed it for food. Everyone ate pigeons when he was young.'

'Urrgh.'

'Would you like a tea?' she asks, switching to English.

'No, too hot,' I reply, in Spanish.

We usually speak like this, always switching between the languages, sometimes sticking to one for whole conversations, then suddenly changing to the other mid sentence - 'What are you doing esta noche?', 'He perdido mis car keys...' - ridiculous, but a completely efficient means of communication.

And I love it when she speaks in English. The sentence 'Do you want a tea?' sounds so gentle when delivered in a soft Spanish accent, far more refreshing than that which it promises.

'Let's go for a walk then,' she says, 'and later I'll cook a nice supper. Venga - wakey wakey - energia!'

Manolo the Hunter

Manolo was the man who would sweep in with his team of freaky extras and transform my flat into something habitable within a matter of weeks. Or so I hoped. He came with the very highest of recommendations from one of my afternoon private students, Maxi, a bank director. Manolo had recently done up Maxi's place and had plumbers, electricians and painters at his fingertips. He was fast, he was efficient, and he was a very fair man. As a special favour Maxi would put me in touch with Manolo and maybe, just for Maxi, he would be able to fit me in.

So it was that I found myself standing in my new flat at the beginning of March with Manolo, his brother, and Marina's mother. Manolo was pacing up and down between the rooms at the front, eulogising about Maxi.

'Maxi is a man of his word, a man of great character, so honest, a very good friend of mine.' He stopped by a window, took a drag on his cigarette, then dropped it and ground it into the dusty tiles. His pinched face, those beady eyes and the micro-moustache clipped tight against the bottom half of his upper lip all broke into a smile. He wore a faded tweed jacket over a striped shirt which opened wide at the neck to reveal a pair of gold chains. He reached into the jacket and pulled out a tape measure and a packet of Marlboro. To all appearances Manolo was 'Costa del Sol' man, the English equivalent of a dodgy car dealer, a clapped out Merc. owner, someone that any self-respecting English hooligan would instantly identify as a 'spic'.

On he went in his gravelly Andalucian accent, dropping the 's's from the end of his words.

'A very great man. Normally I wouldn't take on a small job like this, but as you come recommended by Maxi, and he is a very great friend of mine...' I felt like a mediaeval surf who, on the point of having his land repossessed, is humbly reprieved by a kind word from the bishop. Anyone would think that Maxi was the Mayor of Madrid. It was clear that Manolo was laying down the terms of our engagement: we were bound together by the favour of an honourable man, and as such our business together should be conducted with the utmost respect.

'Well,' he said, ' what sort of work did you have in mind?'

We walked into the kitchen, Marina's mother at the head, then Manolo, closely followed by myself, and the brother, a silent stocky man in a Parka raincoat (like the dodgy car dealer's respectable 'bruvva').

'He would like to put the kitchen in here,' said Marina's mother, leading us into the large room overlooking the *patio* at the back, 'installing the old sink from the current kitchen into the centre of this wall...'

'Uh, actually it was this wall,' I say, but to no avail as Manolo is already directing his brother to measure the space by the window.

'*YO, como el profesional que soy*,' I, as the professional that I am, said Manolo with great relish, 'would suggest you put the sink here.' And it was decided.

In every room the same pattern was repeated, always concluded by Manolo's magic words, delivered with one hand poised in mid-air, a wizard casting forth his spell, '*YO, como el profesional que soy...*'

What could I do? At least his suggestions were sensible: a shower would drain better here, one big radiator better than two small there. Half an hour later, with a final flurry of tape measures and a last few words on the benevolent Maxi, they were gone. A quote for the job would arrive the day after tomorrow.

I went to buy a bed. What use was a flat, regardless of its current condition, without the most rudimentary furniture? I could hardly call myself a home owner if I didn't even possess a bed.

The bed shop occupied a prime corner of the plaza and was governed by a quick-moving man with greying hair and one gruesome, bloodshot eye. He spoke in rapid mumbles whilst shooting around the room, scattering mattresses behind him. My ideal bed was already laid out on display.

'Two metres,' he said, 'that's terribly long, terribly long for a Spanish bed at least. Where do you come from?'

'England.'

'Lovely pillows in England, lovely pillows stuffed with down. Don't get those here, not like in England at least.'

'Will this mattress last?' I asked.

'It will last you forever. Depending of course...' he shot me a mischievous look, 'on what you do in it.'

I went to a local electrical store to look at future light fittings, breaking somewhat prematurely into my home-improving stride. A slight woman behind the counter talked me through her unattractive stock of garish, gold-rimmed lamp shades, then asked me if I lived nearby. I told her that I had just bought a flat around the corner. She smiled and said, 'Welcome to the *barrio*.' I bought a small torch and wished her goodbye.

A few day's later Manolo's quotation arrived. It wasn't cheap, but was honest and meticulously detailed. By removing a few unnecessary things, like new windows in the kitchen, I would be able to keep some costs down. So, he would put in central heating and a new boiler. The kitchen would move to the larger room next door, taking the big old sink with it, but ditching the attractive but entirely impractical old cooking range. A bathroom with shower would be put in where the old kitchen had been, and the old tapless washbasin would be saved, fed by suitable taps plumbed into the wall.

My only regret was that I wouldn't have a bath. Marina's father thought it prudent not to put one in until the building was strengthened at some later stage, in case it fell through the floor. The architect had spoken, and I had to agree. There was a story my grandfather told about a distant uncle who lived in Japan. He had been caught in a block of flats during an earthquake, when the ceiling above suddenly collapsed and a Japanese lady dropped down into the room, still sitting in her bath. He shot out an arm and plucked her to safety, just before the bath plunged on through his floor. Having thus compromised her decency by seeing her naked, he was obliged, as a gentleman, to marry her. So, it was prudent not to mess about with bad floors and baths, especially as the neighbour beneath me was a thick-set, bearded male photographer.

The partition between the two front rooms would be removed to make a large *salon*, with a false ceiling put in to cover the drooping effect caused by the heavy chandeliers. The paper would be stripped from all the walls and the flat would be painted, top to bottom, with standard white paint, NOT bubbly *Gotelet*. Finally the entire place would be rewired, as the current electrical set up looked like it had been put in by an aspiring arsonist.

Thus the flat would maintain most of its original charms whilst being rendered livable-in. Manolo could start, 'as a special favour to Maxi', in two weeks time. He estimated the entire job might take about three weeks. The sooner the better as far as I was concerned. Still living in a room at the hostel, and eating most of my food in the bar opposite, I knew it wouldn't be long before my patience ran out. Now that I had a house, I was desperate to start living in it.

≈

Work started on the eighth of March. Dropping in on my way to work I was pleased to find Manolo decked out in overalls, chief of operations, ordering his minions about with cigarette in hand. He had three men at his disposal. Paco the plumber, a happy, quick-witted man with Manolo's Andalucian accent, a messy crop of greying hair, spectacles, and one extremely cloudy eye. He sorted through his tools while talking me through the work ahead, employing a host of words and expressions that I had never come across before. I nodded and said that it all sounded fantastic.

There was another man with a long, drawn face, a heavy expression and comically drooping eyes. He was in charge of knocking things down and making holes in walls. He just nodded at me whenever I passed, then took up the chisel again. The final member of the crew was a bright-eyed, young South American in backwards baseball cap, whose chief occupation would be to carry all the rubble downstairs.

'Ehhh, Ben!' said Manolo when I arrived. He led me to the front of the flat and thumped the thin partition wall.

'When you come back at lunchtime this will be gone, you will have a beautiful new *salon*, full of light!'

Confident that my flat was in safe, experienced hands, I went off to work. I had just started a new teaching job in a multi-national marketing company. At twelve o'clock, just as I was popping out for a coffee, my mobile rang. It was Manolo.

'Ben, big problems Ben. The neighbours say they will call the police if we continue to work. I have to stop Ben. You better come and talk to them.' My heart sank. I ran for the Metro, thoughts racing, what on earth was going on?

Manolo was standing outside the building when I got there, arguing with two men. As I approached, I caught the magic words flying through the air '*YO, como el professional que soy...*' Oh God.

He was addressing a tall, chubby man with pockmarked skin and a bulbous drinker's nose. The other, a typical nosy neighbour, looked like an ill wolf, with greased back hair and feral eyes. He turned and spoke to me with a coarse lisp.

'If this house falls down and someone dies you'll be put in prison!'

Prison, death, the house falling down? I turned to Manolo who looked at me accusingly and sighed.

'Ben, do you have a *permiso* for the work we are doing?

'A what?' This was the first I had ever heard of such a thing.

'Look,' said bulbous-nose, 'I'm sorry but you are not allowed to do any work in this building. Work on this building has been banned by the council until the main restructural work is completed. Without permission, a *permiso*, you cannot do a thing. We won't report you to the police if you stop now, as you didn't know about it. But obviously if you carry on we'll have no choice.'

I felt like I had been winded. The main restructural work on the building that he was talking about wouldn't even start for another six months at least. I might have to wait over a year before I could continue work on my flat.

A stout, stern-faced old lady arrived on the scene.

'Are you the owner? But what do you think you're doing? I live above you and my God! what a banging this morning! I thought the building was coming down, I thought I'd fall through the floor, I nearly had a heart attack!'

'But, but...' I said, suspended in disbelief, 'I only want to put in a shower and change the electrics, otherwise how am I going to live there? I've bought the flat and all I want to do is to make it habitable...'

'I'm sorry,' said the man with the nose, 'without the *permiso* you cannot do another thing.'

'Well, Ben,' said Manolo, open palms raised to the sky, 'you didn't tell me you didn't have permission. I have my reputation to consider of course, so I will have to stop work immediately. I'm recalling my men. Get to work on the *permiso* as soon as possible, and give me a ring when it's sorted out.'

And he was gone. I went up to see what they had done, shaking from the confrontation, the words prison, heart attack and *permiso* spinning in my mind. What was this damn *permiso*, and why hadn't Manolo, the so-called *profesional,* asked me about it before?

The flat looked like it had been hit by a bombshell. They had indeed knocked down the partition at the front and I did have a lovely big salon. If you ignored the piles of rubble on the floor and the jagged line of broken brickwork along the ceiling and walls then it really wasn't so bad. Lots of light. The plumber had already opened up great crevices in the new kitchen, and carefully twisted tubing lay about ready to be installed. Someone had partly destroyed the old coal-fired cooking range with a heavy, blunt instrument. They had made great progress. The place was a disaster.

I left and wandered the streets in shock. I would never have anywhere to live. I couldn't wait any more. I hadn't been so clever after all. Shit. What had made me think I could just march into a decision like this in a foreign country and expect everything to be O.K.? The clever English bloke had fallen flat on his face, already. I went into a bar that I had never seen before, drank two glasses of red wine to steady my nerves, telephoned Marina from a pay phone in the corner and, on hearing her voice, broke down, overwhelmed by it all.

≈

The council told me that I would have to wait two weeks for the *permiso*. I had given them a form describing what work had to be done on the flat, and would be allowed to go ahead with it if I didn't hear anything from them within that time. No news would most definitely be good news.

To really stir things up there was a meeting of all the building's residents in the meantime, to discuss the restructuring work, the very thing that held the future of my flat in the balance. It took place in a modern council conference hall and was my first opportunity to get a good look at all my new neighbours. There must have been forty of us in total, a full house, and a more motley bunch I have never seen. By the end of the meeting I was convinced that half were insane, a third senile, and the rest powerless in the face of the majority.

Things got under way fairly peacefully. There was a roll call. I was delighted that Marina had come along and could answer for me, that I could hide my Englishness behind her. The council architect who had told me that the building probably wouldn't fall down was chairing proceedings, flanked by her assistant and another, independent architect. Within a minute of her explaining that certain complications had arisen, that one of the flats was owned by a man in Germany who wasn't interested in doing up the building and could thus ruin everything for the lot of us, the place had descended into chaos.

An old woman rose to her feet and started shouting.

'Worms! There are worms in my beams! I live on the ground floor and they are eating my roof, soon the whole place will come down on top of me!' I was still trying to process the information about the man in Germany and the implications this had for me - i.e. no flat ever - while everyone else had taken the old woman's outburst as a cue to launch into a history of their own personal grievances.

'There's a crack the size of a hand in mine, fourth floor, flat D, what are you going to do about it?'

'WHAT?! I've been waiting three years for my balcony to be fixed, I've had enough!'

It was a case of total conversation again, but on a scale I had never previously witnessed. Forty people were complaining at the top of their voices at the same time, accompanied by the constant refrain, a shrill whistle blast above the furore, 'Worms, I've got big fat worms eating my beams!'

The sensible members tried to restore peace by shouting louder than everyone else. The architect and her team screamed, 'Order, order!!' into their microphones, until one of them realised that the microphones hadn't actually been turned on.

I was beginning to feel distinctly edgy, slumped back in my chair, taking in the mayhem. I had practically given up on ever having somewhere to live, but was still pinning some hope on the man with the bulbous nose. He had been listening attentively at the beginning, making sensible comments and taking notes. I looked across to him now, sitting in silence whilst arguments raged to his left and right. Then I noticed that he had started to shake, his fingers fidgeting wildly, his eyes rolling towards the ceiling. Slowly, deliberately, he rose to his feet, picked up his note pad and slammed it down onto the table in front of him. He drew a deep breath and let out a bloodcurdling cry:

'We shall all have to pray to the Virgin of Guadalupe!'

That was the end of that. He turned on his heels and stormed out of the building, followed in dribs and drabs by everyone else. Marina and I went for a drink, not feeling overly optimistic.

≈

The following day my parents arrived in Madrid, took one look at the flat, declared (to my immense relief) that they liked it, then took me away for the weekend. Months before we had booked a room in Valencia, planned to coincide with Las Fallas festivities. If Granada's Las Cruces is a fine example of the Andalucians' love of communal revelry, and the Concurs de Castells of the Catalans' disposition to danger, then Las Fallas shows how each of these typically Spanish characteristics can be taken to extremes. It's not as if the Spaniards are a reckless, lawless people, but there's often a certain laissez-faire approach to their own safety that gives the country a good deal of its charm, that makes me sit back in disbelief and think, 'Only in Spain, this could only happen in Spain.' Never have I felt this more than in Valencia during Las Fallas.

The festival lasts a week, ending each year on March 19th, and demonstrates a local penchant for pyromania. I had been following the fiesta in the newspaper before we left Madrid, as several incidents had filtered through to the national press, mostly involving something called a *Mascleta*.

'What's a *Mascleta*?' I asked one of my students.

'It's a sort of big firework display that they do at lunchtime, it's just supposed to make as much noise as possible. It's a crazy Valencian thing.'

So it seemed. During the week a firework had fallen into a crowd of spectators at one of these events putting fourteen people into hospital, some with wounds to the bone. The casualties were put down to unfortunate collateral damage, certainly no reason to dampen everyone else's fun, and it was business as usual the following day. As soon as we got to Valencia, I knew exactly what I wanted to see, or hear, first and raced off towards the Plaza del Ayuntamiento, Valencia's main square. Loud distant crackles and rumbling booms reverberated around the city, like the sound of distant artillery fire you heard on bulletins during the 1980's conflict in Beirut.

The plaza covered a large open space dotted with palm trees and surrounded by tall elegant buildings. At the centre, in a wide, paved oval area was a seventeen-metre-high papier maché statue of Laurel and Hardy, a *falla*, and next to this a fenced-off area containing fireworks for the *Mascleta*. The council had erected a cordon at a reasonable distance from this, and I took up my position behind it with those already waiting for the two o'clock kick off. Far from discouraging attendance at this potentially lethal event, the local police were allowing as many people to squash into the plaza as possible. By half past one thousands had poured in from the surrounding streets. It was easy to see how one stray firework could cause no end of damage, yet the only safety advice I had seen anywhere had been on the back of a tourist information leaflet in our hotel. It suggested staying away from *Mascletas* if you were pregnant (in case birth was induced), and keeping your mouth open to prevent the noise from bursting your eardrums. My mouth was already open before the thing even started, in disbelief at how many locals had brought along their babies, small children and even pets, all ready to have their delicate hearing damaged for life.

At two minutes to two a terrific whistling started up in the crowd and all eyes were fixed on the centre of the plaza. At two o'clock on the dot, the first rocket went up.

Boooom! It was like a hand-grenade on a stick, quickly followed by another, then four more, then dozens, volley after volley of obscenely loud explosive devices splitting the sky with blasts of noise that rebounded left and right off the plaza's arena of buildings. The bright sunlight took on a curious surreal quality then disappeared behind billowing clouds of smoke. The noise was exhilarating, invigorating, and it was quite extraordinary to be so moved by a firework display that you couldn't even see. After fifteen minutes the *Terremoto*, or earthquake stage commenced. In this, the grand finale, the stakes were upped, quantities doubled. So many of these rocket bombs were going off at once that the atmosphere fizzed, every cell in my body vibrated and the ground actually shook. By the time the smoke cleared several minutes after the end, I was amazed to see the plaza's buildings still standing.

The man next to me was in tears, I think of delight. 'Oh that was a good one, oh what a beautiful one,' he said to his wife, applauding hard like everyone else. We all surged forward to the fenced off zone, wherein a large smiling man with a fat cigar in his mouth was being carried around on somebody's shoulders. He was obviously the orchestrater of this incredible cacophony of sound, doing a lap of honour. We cheered him as an artist, a composer, and I began to understand that this man had put rhythm and tone into all those bangs, creating the most remarkable musical score I had ever heard in my life.

Valencia is a strangely beautiful city. The old town is largely crumbling to the ground, victim of the balmy Mediterranean sea air, yet at any moment you can stumble across beautifully restored churches and gleaming marble plazas. Turn any corner and you may instantly be lost amongst tight grubby back streets, only to emerge later by a leaning minaret to find a neat park full of sprawling Banyan trees.

Most Valencians had taken the week off and there was a wonderful holiday atmosphere in the air, with everybody tossing bangers all over the place, particularly children as young as four, watched over by proud adults. That afternoon, having regrouped after the *Mascleta*, my parents and I wandered amongst the explosive crowds, looking at all of the *fallas*.

These rather garish, enormous papier maché sculptures caricatured famous figures, politicians and film stars, and dominated street corners and plazas. Built during the year by skilled local craftsmen and funded by neighbourhood clubs called *penyas*, they follow a tradition begun in the eighteenth century to celebrate St. Jose's day. Nowadays the *penyas* compete fiercely to come up with the most structurally and satirically ambitious constructions. But what do you think they do with these labours of love when the fiesta comes to an end on March 19th? They burn them down to the ground.

By then the city is tired. Seven days of *Mascletas*, parades, top-grade bullfights, wild *penya* parties, hard drinking and general mayhem have taken their toll. Late on the last day, we set out in search of a suitable *falla* on which to spectate and found ourselves in a small, circular and dilapidated plaza, with a decent *falla* set up near the back. It consisted of two seven metre towers set close together, with Snow White sculpted onto the top on one side. There was a good deal of activity going on around the base so we decided to stay and watch, leaning on the metal barriers that kept us just out of harm's reach.

A man appeared with a tall ladder and a hammer pushed into his belt. He climbed half way up one tower and smashed a head-sized hole in the side. Having done the same at the top, and again on the other tower, he poured large quantities of paraffin into these cavities and propped handfuls of large bangers amongst the *falla*'s internal wooden supports.

'My God,' said my father, 'if they light that thing it'll go up like a rocket.'

'Are you sure this is safe?' said my mother.

'Oh yes, nothing to worry about,' I said, 'we're quite alright behind these barriers.' The barriers were a source of great comfort as quite a large, pushy crowd was building up behind us.

Hammer-man meanwhile was bashing away at the bottom of the structure, followed by a colleague who pushed gallon bottles of paraffin into the spaces he left behind. The firemen arrived, unrolling their hoses before them, and stood around pointing at buildings that seemed particularly at risk. Someone brought out big flat boxes containing ropes of fuse spliced with cardboard explosives, and these were taken up the ladder and draped back and forth between the towers. My mother was worried, my father excited. He had once built a house-high bonfire of wooden pallets for November 5th and created such an inferno that a neighbour had called the fire-brigade. When they arrived, shielding their faces from the heat, they suggested that something more modest might be appropriate in future. Goodness knows what they would have made of this.

The air stank of inflammable liquid and the crowd, now extending back into the side streets, grew restless and began whistling. The firemen put on their helmets, downed their silver visors, and picked up their hoses. At one minute to twelve doors swung open on a first floor balcony to our left. A girl in a neat embroidered green and gold dress stepped out and waved. She was holding a small rocket which she clipped onto a wire that ran from the balcony to the top of the *falla*. At midnight on the dot, she struck a match.

The rocket whizzed across the square and touched off the ropes of explosives strung across the *falla*. These went off with the intensity of extremely close quarter machine gun fire, filling the air with bright white flashes and obscuring the plaza momentarily in clouds of smoke. At the same time - and to our complete horror - the *penya* members ran forward and actually pulled away the barriers in front of us. The paraffin quickly caught fire and flames gnawed away at the papier maché. By the time the bangs subsided there was a pretty substantial fire in front of us, the heat rising quickly. The fireman trained their hoses on the facade of the building just behind the *falla,* in case it should spontaneously ignite. Now there was fire issuing from all levels of the structure, and that low roar that I associate with a really fierce blaze rose from the centre. The heat began to become unbearable. My mother shot me a glance that I understood as 'Ben, this is suddenly extremely silly, there are too many people blocking our path behind,' but the front rows began to concertina backwards and to our immense relief the crowds gave in and let us retreat a few metres.

The flames soon reached their peak, jetting up as high as the eves of the old apartment buildings. Poor Snow White was reduced to glowing embers, and the burning towers broke up into burning shards of wood that tumbled to the ground. The crowd was silent and there was a palpable sadness in the air, the feeling that all the city's capacity for wild fun had gone up in smoke until the same time next year. The firemen, however, soon put an end to this melancholy. They turned their hoses on us and we scattered, hiding round corners in the side streets. From here sorties of young men ran out to taunt the firemen ('come on you big poofs' etc), to be met by a barrage of high-pressure water that soaked them from head to toe.

'Never in my life have I seen anything so ludicrous,' said my father as we made our way back to the hotel, crossing plazas strewn with smouldering ashes. 'That was completely reckless... absolutely marvellous!'

I have yet to see anything in Spain quite so astonishing as the civic irresponsibilities that take place during Las Fallas. There is something wonderfully liberating about the whole thing, that makes you realise how much the British might benefit if the powers that be were just a little less up-tight about health and safety, if the population wasn't pinned down on all sides by thousands of bye-laws, inspectors, 'you can't be too careful's, and petty rules and regulations. Not to the extent that people end up in hospital with bits blown off them, just that they ought to be allowed to get on with enjoying themselves with a little less external control. I've no doubt that the British would be just as care-free as the Valencians, if only they got half a chance. The sensation of vitality and release that comes from being at an event like Las Fallas is invaluable, and can only really be achieved by letting people go just that little bit too far if they want to. It is a tonic, like smelling salts or a stiff drink. It leaves you feeling alive and fully refreshed. After that weekend in Valencia I was ready for anything, fully prepared for whatever disaster the flat business had in store for me next.

≈

Ten days had passed, then at last two weeks, and by some miracle I hadn't heard a thing from the council. I had permission, the elusive *permiso*, and the work could go ahead. A fortnight later Manolo was back on the job with the same team. Every day I approached the flat warily, waiting to be leapt upon by neighbours baying for English blood. I would climb the stairs, averting my eyes from each floor's giant cracks, then enter the flat to check up on the day's latest demolitions.

Manolo would greet me with his familiar cry, 'EH, Ben! Come and see what we've done!' before launching into an attack on my taste.

'I wish you'd let us put a new floor over these nasty tiles... why do you want to keep this ridiculous old sink... in my flat, ahhhh Ben, you should see my flat Ben, in my flat I have multi-coloured wall tiles all over the bathroom walls, something to keep in mind... why on earth won't you let us throw out this leaky washbasin, it doesn't even have any taps!' I was dubbed *El Rustico*, and he simply assumed that the British were not a particularly progressive race.

After a while I began to relax. Most of the plumbing was in place, much of the rubble had gone, the hole-making man had stripped out most of the old electrics, ready to be replaced. I was getting on with Manolo and his gang, avoiding the neighbours, and learning a whole new vocabulary: *Rozas* were the great channels dug into the walls for pipes and wiring. *Cabe* meant 'it fits', or 'well, it it'll just about go in there'. Then one morning I dropped in and met the tiler, a cocky young man who took after his uncle, Manolo. He had come to put in some tiles behind the shower basin.

'The floors are shit,' he told me, 'the ceilings worse. This place won't last you know.' He got on with his work, I tried to dismiss him as an idiot but it was too late, once again the seeds of doubt were sown. Had I really bought the right flat?

And then I met the *escayolista*, the false ceiling man, who was to cover the original drooping ceilings in the salon. He looked as if he had just walked off the set of an old French spoof, wearing white overalls made whiter still by a complete splattering of plaster, and a white cap from below which thick strawy black hair poked out at the sides. His forearms and hands were snow-white (plaster again), and finally, to round off the effect, below his big black moustache he chewed a big fat black cigar, bits of which he bit off between sentences and spat onto the floor.

'*Muy mal, muy mal*', very bad, very bad, he said as soon as I arrived, 'the floors are very bad.' Here we go again, I thought. 'And the ceilings, poff, completely fucked. And I should know.' He wandered over to the balcony and peered out of the open doors. 'Of course the outside of the building, the facade, isn't too bad, but, well, the inside is a disaster. Demolition. The best thing would be demolition, just knock it all down and start again.' You can imagine with what joy I welcomed this latest assessment.

I wasn't prepared, however, to let him get to me.

'Isn't there *anything* that can be done?' I was looking for at least one optimistic opinion.

'Well,' he said, 'the beams aren't bad. In fact they will certainly last another hundred years, or more. Really it's just that the wood has bowed. It looks terrible. It's the same throughout the centre of Madrid.' So that was it, a matter of aesthetics. The curvature of the floor and ceilings *looked* terrible, nothing more, but reason enough in his eyes for the complete demolition of the building. No doubt he lived in a brand-new, ninety-degree flat in the north of the city.

To round all this off there was the encounter with the bald, toothless painter, never seen without a roller in his hand, decorating his head with white spots.

'The walls are terrible,' he said, 'A disaster, full of defects. I'll never get them perfect.'

'Oh, really?' I replied, getting used to this by now.

'Dynamite!' he said, 'the best hope for this building is dynamite.'

'Come on,' I said, 'is it really so bad?'

'Well, I mean, I have actually worked on restructuring buildings like this in the past. Buildings much worse than this actually.'

'And?'

'And actually it is possible to completely strengthen these old places without the occupants even having to move out. They'll last forever then you know.'

In my mind, a theory was starting to take shape, a Spanish-ism perhaps. I would call it 'Short term total pessimism syndrome,' or 'anti-optimism,' being the condition of always considering all possible outlooks, then seeking from these the most extremely negative conclusion available, and resigning oneself to this with a very heavy heart. The Spanish, I decided, were a people of extremes, dynamite or delight (and usually dynamite). Only when gently coaxed might they reluctantly arrive at a more optimistic, realistic appraisal of a given situation. It's absolutely infuriating.

≈

The work finished, though I was hard pressed to believe it, at the end of April, a little outside Manolo's original estimate of 'about three weeks'. We met at the flat to go over the final bill. He was back in his tweed jacket again, all smiles and charm. We made a quick tour of inspection, he conceding that he had actually carried off the *rustico* look to great effect. We finished up in the living room, which was indeed large and light, and filled with the presence of the trees.

'Ah, Ben. Do you know what I like to do at the weekends?' He guided me by the arm to the window.

'No, what?'

'Well, I like to go hunting, hunting Ben.'

'Oh, really?' It seemed a strange time for a man-to-man.

'My brother and I drive out into the wild with our guns, and shoot whatever we can find. It is the most relaxing way to spend a weekend.' He pulled out a cigarette and lit it. 'Right, come on, let's have a look at this bill.'

If he was trying to gently suggest that I give him no trouble in paying, he needn't have worried. The sooner I got shot of that lot, putting an agonising month behind me, the better.

Manolo the hunter. The idea of him walking around the Spanish countryside with a rifle was quite alarming, enough to keep me away from the hills for good. I gave him his cheque, he ground his cigarette into the tiles for the last time, said a final few well chosen words on Maxi, and was gone.

The flat was habitable, the building still standing, and the relief immeasurable. It had been another whirlwind, but at last everything had unfolded as planned. I moved out of the hostel and into my flat, where now I sit, jumping up every now and again to look for cracks in the paint work, between writing these lines.

19th July 2001

As I come out of the Metro on my way into work I see oily clouds of smoke devouring the sky above the district of Goya. I think, 'another bomb.' I hurry to the office where a small crowd of staff and visitors have gathered round the television. One of the receptionists produces the slim ergonomic remote control from beneath her desk and the volume is turned up.

Early news reports do little to clarify the situation. Aerial views of smoke engulfing what appears to be a vast chunk of the city are mixed freely with telephone updates from the site of the bomb. It must have been massive. Ten minutes later we see other shots of a destroyed bank and paramedics ministering to people on the ground and the confusion begins to clear. There has been an attempt on someone's life in one corner of the city, whilst in another a stadium has caught fire.

The bomb exploded around eight o'clock this morning in a quiet barrio in the north, seriously injuring an army brigadier and several passers by, and shattering windows and brick-work in surrounding buildings. Meanwhile the city's main sporting venue has burnt down. A welder accidentally ignited the roof whilst fixing it up for tonight's performance of Riverdance (the show is cancelled, what a terrible blow to Madrid's cultural agenda). Only two people have been hurt, one from smoke inhalation - incredible that it wasn't more, considering the quantity of smoke - and the other a fireman who fell five metres from a ladder.

Like the news people we had all assumed at first that the two incidents were one, that the billowing palls of smoke erupting above the city were due to the latest work of the Basque terrorists ETA. As the smoke rose, visible from all corners of the capital, our fear was that this time the explosion had been on a catastrophic scale.

The bombed brigadier, ETA's intended target, is alive, though seriously injured. The device was strapped to a bicycle propped against a lamp-post, a new development for ETA, who normally use car-bombs. A neighbour phones in to the television to report that everyone in the victim's building knew this might happen one day, that *they knew exactly what had happened the moment they heard the explosion. We see some blood on the road, the usual unpleasant shots typical of Spanish television.*

I make a quick tour of the building. 'No class today,' says my most reliable student, 'I am too tired from all this news to speak English.' That's a new one, usually they don't even bother with excuses anymore, just a 'not today,' or 'impossible.' I decide to give up on the others and go home, seeing wisps of smoke slowly fading over Goya as I duck down into the Metro.

Under a Spanish Sun

Some Madrileños say that Lavapies is the last real *barrio* community in Madrid. Generations have lived in the same buildings, people greet each other by name on the streets and ask about each other's cousins in the local surgery. When an old man died in our building a notice was put up in the foyer inviting all the neighbours to the wake. The population is denser here than anywhere else in the city, with several hundred thousand people jumbled on top of each other in an area far smaller than my childhood four-hundred person village. This can make the tight streets seem claustrophobic at times, especially after a weekend in the countryside. Mostly though it is a comforting, lively place, home to grocers, butchers, clock makers and furniture restorers, and one of Madrid's most vibrant districts on a Saturday night (God knows how many bars there are in Lavapies).

With Manolo gone I moved into the *barrio* at last, feeling rather pleased about taking my place in one of the city's most beautiful old quarters. As I had gathered at the residents meeting, most of my building's occupants were pensioners, who lived in run-down but neatly furnished flats. Neighbours stopped to chat on the stairs and there was a strong sense that the *communidad*, the association of neighbours of which I had become a part, was indeed a proud, contented community. The concept of *communidad* also encompassed the bricks and mortar of the building, the interior *patios*, the corridors and the stairwell, areas we expected each other to treat with the same degree of respect afforded to our own homes. Soon after I arrived this was made quite clear in a photocopied note placed into everybody's letter box. It read as follows:

'During many years this building has been characterised by the peaceful, happy cohabitation of its neighbours; however, for some time we have had to put up with a lack of civility on the part of certain undesirables who have no place in this block, but belong instead in a pigsty or a stable. Pigs (they have no other name) spit on the floor. Bags of rubbish are left on top of the bins before they are put out. Cigarette butts and bits of paper litter the corridors. Dogs and cats wander around as they please, pissing and shitting all over the place.

These are just a few examples of an untenable situation against which severe measures must be taken if we are to eradicate these problems for good. We want to live in peace, respecting a few basic rules of cohabitation and avoiding all these aggravations!

'This is a COMMUNITY OF NEIGHBOURS where certain simple norms of behaviour exist: these are called MANNERS!

'Signed: the majority of the neighbours.'

I certainly didn't remember signing anything, but thought I probably was on the side of decency and didn't remember having ever spat on the floor. I presumed that the culprits were the druggy looking types who rented flats on a couple of floors and drank cheap lager in the plaza all day. Still, anything was possible. It wouldn't be the first time that I had slipped up on the manners front as a foreigner living in Spain.

On the domestic side, for example, table manners have proved a minefield from which I seldom emerge unscathed. Woe betide the hapless Englishman who has one hand in his lap whilst eating his soup with the other. The offending hand must be placed at rest on the table next to the bowl. And while we are on soup, remember never, ever to dip your bread into it in polite company.

'We will let you dip your bread today, as we are at home,' said Marina's mother when she first caught me in the act.

Beyond the dinner table there is the etiquette minefield surrounding just who's paying for what and when. Here, it seems, I'm constantly at fault. Whilst one week I'm part of an enlightened and emancipated couple wherein I should never expect to pay more than my own fair share, I will be reprimanded the next for failing to buy an appropriate round of drinks.

'It's a question of *educacion*,' manners, says Marina, that word cropping up again, instantly evoking a complex Spanish behavioural code with which I'm supposed to be fully *au fait*.

'Don't worry... it's just another cultural misunderstanding thing,' I reply, wheeling out my all-weather excuse.

These international mismatches were not, however, always so easily reconciled. Having settled into the flat, I really hoped that it wouldn't be long until Marina moved in. We had talked about it in the past and agreed that one day it would be a great idea, whenever she felt ready and, of course, only if her parents would agree. Unfortunately this seemed highly unlikely. If staying the night was deemed unethical, then cohabiting before marriage would be down right demonic, no matter how we felt or what went on where I came from.

This really got my hackles up, not just because it seemed that my moral rules counted for nothing, but also because of a new, significant realisation. I had to face the fact that, no matter how lucky I was to be living a wonderful life beneath a bright Spanish sun, I had made a disturbingly long-term commitment.

I had bought a house, something I always expected to do not too far from where I started out in life, and certainly not on the other side of the continent, let alone in Madrid. A cousin once told me how lucky I was to be living a different, interesting life that most of my contemporaries could never know. True enough. But then I thought about their parallel, normal adult life, the one that I would otherwise be living back in the UK, and might now never know. Would I in fact be the one missing out by never experiencing that? And there was (and often still is), a sense of guilt too, about everybody I had distanced myself from, the missed family and friends.

All this amounted to a feeling of slight panic once I had moved in and sat down to think about things. For a while I felt like I had made a giant gamble by buying the flat. Based on a love for Spain, and of course for Marina, I had changed my life for good. I began to believe that only when she moved in beside me would I be able to calm down and consider that the bet had been a safe one after all. I was quite impossible for a while.

'Speak to your parents!' I said, 'when do you think they might let you move in?'

'*AY*, Ben!' she would reply, 'Leave me in peace! I'll speak to them after the summer. You have to remember that this isn't England. You are living in Spain! This is their country and you have to live by their rules! And anyway, what about me? Maybe I'm quite happy where I am at the moment.'

'Oh.'

At the beginning of May I went away for a long weekend with Al, providing Marina with some peace. Travelling again to a different part of Spain, leaving Madrid for a while, pure escapism, within the grand scheme of escapism that is my life in Spain.

≈

I picked Al and Gail up at nine o'clock on Friday night, once they had finished work. We were heading for Andujar, a small town just before Cordoba, at the edge of the Sierra Morena mountains. Gail, another T.E.F.L. friend, thirty something, bright eyed and ever-enthusiastic, had once lived there and had invited us along to see the town's *Romeria*, a pilgrimage that takes place there at the end of April each year. As at the outset of any trip down to Andalucia, we were all in high spirits.

'Will there be Sevillanas dancing?' asked Al.

'Oh yes, plenty of Sevillanas, this lot are absolutely mad,' said Gail.

'Excellent,' said Al, 'there's nothing in the world like a good Andalucian Sevillanas fiesta.'

We drove south through the star-studded darkness, stopping briefly at an isolated turn-off to stretch our legs and taste the air.

'So what are your friends like then Gail?' asked Al.

'Bonkers actually.' We kicked about in the roadside scrub for a while, releasing strong scents of rosemary and wild thyme, images of crazed dancing and wild abandon swimming in my mind.

We arrived at half past one, driving into what seemed to be a rather dead and not particularly interesting, scruffy modern town. There was barely anyone to be seen.

'Don't worry,' Gail reassured us, 'all the action takes place in the old town.'

We parked the car and went in search of her friends, who were said to be around somewhere, drinking. Strolling down empty streets, past featureless apartment blocks, we came at last to an older, open plaza, in one corner of which a small group of people stood next to some deserted trestle tables at which there had obviously been a makeshift bar. 'Gail!' they shouted as we approached, and welcomed us with enthusiastic kisses and hand shaking.

There was Alan, forty-ish, English, and terribly friendly, whose wife was local, pretty faced, and kept close to his side. And Ana, a stout lady in a wide-brimmed black Andalucian hat, with white shirt and braces, and a wild, naughty drunken smile. And there was Juani, perhaps drunker still, and her boyfriend, another local man, who was the drunkest of them all.

'Have we arrived too late?' I asked, hoping that there would be something more than this after an exhausting four-hour drive.

'No, no,' said Alan, 'we were just waiting for you lot, come on, lets go.'

And off we went, deeper into the dilapidated old town, emerging later in a larger plaza, where the air was warm and where, beneath the glowing honey-coloured walls, all our worries disappeared.

The place was teeming with life. Magnificent dappled grey horses ridden by excited young boys were parading up and down, lurching alarmingly towards encouraging crowds. Proud, dark, powerful-featured women gossiped in groups, wearing long, colourful polka-dot Sevillanas dresses, whilst the men stood apart, smoking hard, held straight in their tight waistcoats beneath deep rimmed hats and staring eyes. Those children who hadn't got hold of a horse, or weren't doing their best to get trampled underneath one, danced around, weaving in and out of adult legs, none showing the least sign of fatigue.

At one end of the Plaza the crowd was thickest, bunting dipped back and forth across a long open air bar, whilst the commotion of music and movement meant only one thing: Sevillanas. We got a drink and stood and watched the dancing couples step in and out of a close invisible sphere, backs arched, one hand held high in the air, eyes transfixed on the others', side-stepping their partners in bold, spinning turns.

'A million people are going up the mountain outside town tomorrow,' said Alan, 'they either go up on foot, on horse back, or in covered trailers. Then they stay up there for two days, eating and dancing Sevillanas like this at the foot of the Virgin's church. We'll probably just drive up to the half way stage with everyone else, just below the mountains, where the Pilgrims stop to eat on the way.'

'Why do they go up to the church?' I asked.

'The figure of the Virgin, the *Virgin de la Cabeza,* is up there.'

'And what's so special about the Virgin?'

'They hid her from the Moors when they invaded Spain, then a few centuries later a shepherd boy saw lights and heard bells coming from beneath a pile of rocks and he found the figure of the Virgin. This shepherd had a crippled arm, and by the time he had carried the Virgin back down to the the town it was cured. So, they built her a church up on the hill where he had found her, and now they all troop up there every year.'

There is hardly a fiesta in Spain that doesn't somehow involve the Moorish invasion, a figure of the Virgin or, come to think of it, a shepherd.

Early the following morning, with memories of other plazas, too much *Fino* and some *discoteca* appearing through the haze, we set off out of town. We drove along a small, winding road, empty fields turning quickly into a sumptuous, folding landscape of deep green banks, bursting with tall grasses and splashes of bright wild flowers. Tall, bushy Eucalyptus trees lined the route, while shallow streams scattered themselves across smooth rocks below horseshoe bridges. It was the stuff of dreams again, an intangibly perfect picture, made real and opened up for us to drive along by some kind twist of fortune.

The place where we had decided to spend the day was even better than the journey to it. This, the halfway stage on the pilgrimage from the town to the Chapel, consisted of a series of fields set along a shallow river, fields stained deep purple by a single strain of lilac flower that flourished beneath broad, stunted oaks. Behind, on the last and lowest peak of a corroded, sun-dried sierra, stood the large white-washed chapel where the figure of the Virgin was kept.

Following Alan, Ana and the others, Al and I parked up beside a tree. A folding table appeared, and a feast was slowly laid out: ham, *tortilla*, chicken, *empanadas*, beans, cheeses, wine and, of course, the inevitable *Fino*. A great pall of smoke was rising behind the chapel high up on the hill.

'That's the fire,' said Alan 'they throw candles and bunches of flowers onto it constantly as a tribute to the Virgin. The caravans will be coming over the river soon, let's go and have a look.'

We wandered down towards the river, past other happy picnickers, past full legs of ham hanging mockingly from the trees (the best *Iberico*-ham pigs, during the last year of their lives, roam freely beneath these oaks, foraging on acorns). Two women stepped away from one table carrying a strange contraption comprising two hoops joined by a bundle of cloth. Stopping a few metres away and dropping this on the grass, one stepped into the middle whilst the other lifted a hoop up above her friend's head, forming a tall, broad tube of cloth. The friend in the middle ducked down into this and disappeared.

'Andalucian Porta-loo!' said Alan.

As we reached a long, arched stone bridge, I noticed a curious, colourful procession snaking slowly down a small hill beyond.

'Look,' said Ana, 'Let's wait for them here.'

And one by one what looked like those old gypsy caravans from children's tales, with arched open backs and bright striped roofs, rattled down and across the bridge towards us, pulled along at a mourning pace by colourfully decorated tractors. Each caravan held about twenty people dressed in fine suits and Sevillanas dresses, shouting, '*Viva la Virgin! Viva la Virgin de la Cabeza!*' A man at the front carved delicate strips off a leg of ham, and those swinging their legs off the back passed bottles of *Fino* and wine skins around. The procession that came down from that hill looked so pleasure driven and pagan that anyone who arrived without being forewarned would have been hard pushed to pick out the religious element in the whole affair.

'This lot come first, eighty-odd caravans in all,' explained Alan, 'then the horses arrive, hundreds of horses, and finally those on foot.'

As the caravans took up position in the surrounding fields for lunch, Al and I, after reeling off a few photos, were forced to take our leave. A return trip to Granada awaited at the end of the day. We had overplanned, for now I longed to stay another night and head up to the chapel with the revellers after lunch, to be there in the evening when the horse riders arrived, to dance the night away in the glow of that mighty flower-fueled fire.

'At least you're leaving before the others,' said Alan, 'the police turn a blind eye today and sooner or later everyone else who's come up here by car heads down to town and well, you can imagine, they're all completely drunk by then.'

The police turning a blind eye to hundreds of drunk drivers, I thought, as we weaved the car amongst the happy revellers... only in Spain.

We drove back down towards the town, transfixed by what we had seen, and by the return along that dreamy road. I felt incredibly happy. At last, I realised, I was really starting to find out what was down at the end of all those little Spanish roads.

What's more, when I think about it now, I see what that intangible, dream element to these travels through Spain may actually be. I have a clearer idea about the ecstasy of travel, that which I had glimpsed on the train to Seville, or whilst gazing across to the Alhambra Palace at sunrise. It is as though we are seeing our imagination bettered, turned into something real and presented directly to us. In this case I was driving down what I then considered to be a road more beautiful than I could imagine, a road so beautiful in fact that it could only be a figment of the imagination. Yet there it was. It is when we pass through these solid swathes of real, perfect imagination, that we become perfectly content, not only because these scenes are so wonderful to behold, but also because we have finally fulfilled our reason for travel, and entirely escaped the ordinary world for a while.

≈

A few months later, in November, much to my amazement Marina suddenly moved in. Not because I had finally harangued her into it - I had calmed down a bit by then - but, incredibly, because her parents had actually suggested it. In fact they told her over the summer that they thought she should move in at the beginning of that autumn, straight after the holidays. God knows how they came to that conclusion. She decided, however, that November would do quite nicely instead. So we planned a trip to Lisbon, a romantic, pre-cohabitation weekend.

I had almost got over the initial shock of living in my very own Spanish flat by then, and I felt really quite happy about everything. About Marina coming to live with me, about my bricks-and-mortar investment. I was building up a good collection of photos from around the country and doing a bit of writing. All seemed well. Right up, that is, until the point when she was an hour from actually moving in, until the moment I saw the stabbed woman.

By November, all the leaves had gone from the trees at the windows. The evening skies were often grey, and once the sun went down it was soon cold. We came back from Portugal on a Sunday afternoon, and Marina went to her parents' house to collect some belongings before the final, definitive move. I came back to the flat to straighten things up, to try and breathe heat and life into the place.

At about ten past six, with the light failing and the line-drawn branches of the trees shifting uneasily above the street, I heard screams from children. They weren't the screams of a game. Looking out of the window I saw a terrified group of boys and girls run into the bargain international calls shop just up the road, all staring back down the street as they pushed their way through the door.

I looked down the road and saw a woman. She was motionless, doubled up, lying on her side with her back to me, wearing a fawn raincoat, some stuffed shopping bags at her side. Above her stood a short man with a small kitchen knife in his hand, arms limp by his side.

Two men ran out of the bar below shouting '*HIJO DE PUTA*,' picking up bags of rubbish and hurling them at him. I felt a jolt of shock and ran to the phone.

'Don't come yet!' I said to Marina.

'Why not?'

'Nothing. Something bad. Outside. Just don't come until I phone you.'

I ran back to the window. Should I phone the police? No, there were people on the balconies opposite already using their phones. Now the man who had been holding the knife was flat out on his back, next to the woman, both motionless, people crowding around. Someone had obviously knocked him down. There was something too unreal about his; this was something that only ever happened in films.

A few minutes passed before the ambulances came. She still hadn't moved. She was dead, of course she was, stabbed to death in the street below my flat. Who was she? The man with the knife roused himself, trying to lift himself up, but another man put a foot firmly on his chest and shouted '*TE QUEDAS ALLÍ!*' You stay there.

The police arrived and pushed the man into the back of their car, whilst women crowded around the door and shouted '*CABRON!*' Bastard. They spat at him and drew their fingers slowly across their throats.

Was she dead? Three ambulances came. The paramedics ministered to her on the ground for a while, bandaging her, then they picked her up and put her on a trolley. They pushed her up the hill towards an ambulance, passing right below my windows, right beneath my feet, where she suddenly raised one arm, then let it flop down again at her side. Thank God, I thought, she's alive.

Twenty minutes later there was nothing, no-one standing about and gossiping, no police or ambulances, nothing in fact but a crumpled surgical glove on the pavement. People walking past the spot where she fell would never know that anything had happened. It makes you wonder. How many more things do we miss in life, as endless events, good and bad, are drawn into the landscape and disappear?

(The papers, who partly resolve this problem in our lives, spoke the next day of a Portuguese woman and a jealous partner who stabbed her in the arm, the stomach, and the back, as she tried to move out of their house. Her condition was described as *grave*.)

A few hours later, Marina moved in. Into the lethal streets of Lavapies.

It didn't help that the following Sunday, a warm sunny morning this time, a small scale riot came rumbling down the street. I was screwing together a kitchen cabinet in the *salon*, last weeks stabbing almost cleared from my mind, when I heard the most almighty, splintering crash of broken glass. Up at the balcony again (all life passes below my feet), I saw a crowd of balaclava-ed youths come rolling down the street, wine bottles in their hands. They had tipped a brimming bottle bank into the road and they were using the bottles to smash the glass in the phone booths below the flat. They kept on coming, smashing and crashing, keen student photographers snapping away in their wake. Then came the riot police, keeping their distance, pump action super-guns pointing up at the sky. What the hell was going on this time? The TV told us later: it was the anniversary of Franco's death and these were anti-fascist demonstrators, which somehow didn't seem quite right.

I wondered whether I would ever get any peace, whether cultural misunderstandings, self-flagellating sentiments of displacement and urban chaos would ever let me sit back, see where I had got to, and actually relax.

22nd July 2001

Things seem to be clearing up in my mind. By the end of the month, I should be more certain. I should be able to pin things down, to be really sure about what exactly it is that I think is going to happen next.

I've started walking to work again, down past Atocha and through the Retiro Park. I've got no excuse not to in this weather, but really it's because I can't stand the Metro any longer. As July draws to a close, the trains are still packed tight every morning and I just can't cope anymore. Why travel to work pressed tight up against some overweight businessman's sweaty back if there's a decent alternative?

This morning the entrance to the park is almost deserted. A couple of dogs mope about, a homeless man is still asleep between too bushes at the edge of the grass. It is hot. The temperatures haven't dipped below twenty degrees during the night, and already, at half past eight, they are edging their way back up again. I cut through a grove of towering horse chestnuts, into the dusty open area where the South Americans gather for impromptu barbecues, football, and drinking on Sundays. Beneath one of the low trees that form long avenues across this empty space, a young man is working a bright magenta and yellow bullfighting cape, describing long slow turns, the cloth held rigidly out in front, feet rooted firmly to the ground, eyes never once breaking contact with the imaginary bull as it blasts past him, wheels round, and disappears beneath the cape again.

I pass the lake, where a solitary oarsman skulls lazily towards me, occasionally pulling the blades from the water and drawing them back through the air. Beyond the lake, amongst the trees, they are watering the grass. Thick jolting jets erupt from stand pipes to cast dripping, golden arcs of light where the sun reaches beneath the leafy canopies to illuminate the spray.

As I walk I'm scuffing my feet on the path and thinking about this book, about the weather, about what has happened since Marina moved in, about anything but the meeting that's coming up on Thursday. I saw the sign this morning, taped to our building's front door. It said, 'Meeting of the residents, last Thursday in July. To further discuss renovations to the structure of the building.' Oh no, not again.

Radio Bellas Artes

Winter brought a great chill, an icy frigidity that swept down from the sierra and engulfed the streets in air as bitterly cold as the summers are impossibly hot. (Only briefly in spring and autumn does the climate alternate between these extremes, when it rains and it blows, and the city really doesn't seem to be Madrid anymore.) Up in the mountains in winter the landscape is barely recognisable. Within an hour of Madrid's city centre, you are at 2000 meters, careering though classic alpine scenery on skis, or bumping downhill in a toboggan. The snow sits neck deep at the road side, and the half-buried, Christmas-card pine forests bathe in icy sunshine and resonate with a comforting, muffled silence.

The New Year began beneath grey skies, more cold, and heavy rain. An entire apartment building came crashing to the ground in the smart western zone of Arguelles. By some miracle it was empty, cleared for restructuring work, and only two people died, a workman, and a homeless person who had sought refuge somewhere on the ground floor. A few weeks later it happened again, though this time only half a building collapsed, somewhere near the Plaza Mayor. The council blamed the rain for undermining foundations, whilst the local press blamed immigrant workers, who didn't know not to hit supporting walls with sledge-hammers.

The corridors of my building came to life with speculation and worry again: would it happen to us? When was our restructuring work due to begin, and who would they employ to do it? Marina and I decided that we would move out quickly, just in case, the moment they eventually started work on the building. It was almost a year since I had bought the house, however, and there was still absolutely no sign of the plan of reforms that Pilar had promised.

But it was just possible not to worry too much about the building falling down if you ignored the worst of the gossips on the stairs. Marina and I, meanwhile, were happily living together, doing our best to accommodate the more infuriating elements of each other's domestic education.

'Ben,' she would say, 'can you take down the rubbish?'

'I'm sure it can wait until tomorrow. In England the dustbin men only came once a week.'

'Well, this is Madrid so they come every night.'

'Yes, yes, but I really can't be bothered.'

'Oh well, neither can I. Let's just forget it.'

My work at the multi-national marketing place continued apace although I sometimes wondered whether it actually qualified as 'work' at all. I spent a lot of time just sitting in the top floor canteen, looking out of the window and thinking how nice the view would be if all the city's buildings disappeared, leaving nothing but deep blue sky and the rocky hills that once lay underneath. 'What am I doing here, stuck in this bloody office block?' I would think. The job was not overly taxing.

Each morning I arrived at nine and waited for my first student to turn up, normally about twenty minutes late. 'Sorry,' they would generally say and then, repeating a well-worn phrase, 'no English today, I have a meeting in fifteen minutes.' Every hour I would make a quick tour of the building to check on my next victim, ascertain that they too were busy ('Sorry, too much work... a report to finish... too tired... don't feel like it today...') then head back to the canteen or out to a nearby park. I worked four mornings a week, and nearly always went home before my official two o'clock finish, paid for five hours of work and done practically nothing.

The excuse most often used for getting out of my classes was 'I didn't leave the office until x o'clock last night.' I heard tales of entire teams working to finish a project until midnight, even three o'clock in the morning, and on occasion some students said that they had rushed back into the office at nine after only two hours sleep. Didn't they have rights? Shouldn't they be getting overtime for all this? I had a vague memory that in England pens were downed at six o'clock on the dot, when everyone went straight home or to the pub, and woe betide the boss that tried to stop them.

I thought for a while that the Spanish were simply working incredibly hard to catch up with richer European countries like England, France or Germany, but things weren't quite as simple as that.

'Stupid macho Spanish rubbish,' said an English teacher I knew, 'it's like a competition, especially with the men. Who can outdo who and stay the latest. My husband is a management consultant and I never see him before ten o'clock at night. I'm fed up with it, keep telling him to get another job, but it probably wouldn't make any difference.'

Laura, a student, told a different story. 'What can you do? If all your work-mates are staying you have to stay too. No-one is going to be the first to get up and leave if there is still work to be done, it looks bad, and you know, it's bad manners.'

Having slunk off early again I would be thankful that I worked free-lance, and not as a standard company employee. Even against the usual twenty-four-hour-a-week English teaching timetables, I was sure that I now had the cushiest contract in Madrid, and I couldn't see myself giving it up for some time.

With a reliable income and the presence of Marina, life in Lavapies began at last to take on a semblance of normality. The only thing that seemed to be suffering was the photography. Al and I found that the shorter days and live-in girlfriends were eroding away at our photographic trips away. *Extranjeros* Out of Focus was all but a thing of the past, especially since half the members had left - Jackie had moved to Vietnam and Matt's whereabouts were unknown. Having thus lost a valuable motive for mid-week drinking, we quickly found another ruse for getting together once a week on cold winter evenings. Real Madrid were doing particularly well in the Champion's League football tournament, as usual, and conveniently played on Tuesday or Wednesdays. Off we went to the bars of Alonso Martinez where we met up with Stephen, and Mike, another Englishman who had started work with Al at my old academy.

Our route never wavered. We began at a long thin bar on Calle Fernando VI where the football was always on, blaring out of a TV pinioned above the door to the street. There was never anyone else in there but a large old man with an ailing Alsatian, and a young, wiry Madrileño who hovered nervously at the end of the bar and impressed us by drinking between three and four substantial gin and tonics before the end of every game. We drank beer from bottles and made sure to order *chupitos*, shots of brandy, coke and a liquor called 'The 43', before we left, as they were always on the house.

The football out of the way, we made straight for an old favourite, the Fino Bar. One such evening, at the beginning of February, we were surprised to look in through the window and see the place half full of customers. Like most of the bars in the area it was usually empty until the weekends.

'Hello, my friends!' said Julian, as we walked in. Julian was the owner, a middle-aged Spaniard with sun wrinkled features, a dark mop of hair, and a wiry black moustache. He was sitting behind the bar on a high stool, with a guitar across his lap and the familiar whiskey and soda in front of him.

'Tonight we have music!' he said, 'here, Mike, come on, play us something.'

'No, no, no,' said Mike, 'maybe a bit later.'

Mike played in a band and as such had been coerced into taking up Julian's guitar in the past, surprising us all by playing Brazilian Bossanovas and singing along in Portuguese.

Julian's wife, a tall blond woman, was standing next to us at the bar, smiling as usual. Behind, in a corner, was an enormous, sweaty man drinking something-and-coke and stuffing olives into his mouth. By the fruit machine on the other side of the room, where long ago I'd been hit by Marina's olive bones, were a group of girls. One looked half Indian, two were chubby, round faced and obviously sisters, and the last was a beautiful girl with cropped blonde hair curled under her chin, small black glasses, and a thin waist squeezed into a tight white cotton top. Julian produced four glasses and filled them with dark, treacley Oloroso wine.

'A present,' he said, then turning to the girl in the cotton top, 'so, Rocio, what's it to be next?'

'Sevillanas!' she said, and Julian began strumming out the lively triplets on his guitar. The sisters and the fat man immediately started beating time with their palms, CLAP clap clap, CLAP clap clap, and Al just had time to put his drink down before Julian's wife pulled him into the middle of the room for the first part of the dance. Rocio's voice sailed across the bar, filling the room with soft musical phrases - *'El dia que yo me muera, que no me llorre Sevilla'* - that rose like tides, welling up above the guitar and the clapping into high rippling tones that she sang with her eyes tight shut and her hands on her hips.

Mesmerised by the voice and the music Mike, Stephen and I leant back and watched Al dancing. The song rose towards the final, fourth part - *'y mi madre y mi hijo quieren a toda mi familia'*, CLAP clap clap - and I was grinning and stamping my foot in time to the claps until Rocio and Julian brought the song to a sudden, cascading end and we all cheered and applauded and beseeched Rocio for more.

'No, that's it, we've got to go, really...'

'Come on, sing us the English one,' said Julian.

'You must be joking!' said Rocio, looking at the four of us.

'Come on,' we said.

'Rocio, it's the most beautiful song you sing, your best, please, please sing it for us,' said Julian, and she wavered for a minute, pulled her stool into the middle of the bar and began, unaccompanied by the guitar.

Never would I have thought it possible for one of my least favourite songs to be transformed into something so moving, yet half way through the Whitney Houston theme to The Bodyguard I thought I might even be close to tears. The 'I-ai-I... will always love you' floated so gently through the room that no one moved a muscle, and it wasn't until some minutes after she had finished that I felt quite normal again. It must have been the alcohol. Rocio and her gang left after that, off to another bar with Julian's wife and the fat man in tow.

'More Oloroso?' said Julian.

'No,' said Al, 'four beers.' These he produced, with a small plate of olives and pickled onions. He sat down opposite us on his stool and topped up his whiskey and soda with a bottle he kept separate under the bar.

'When I was younger it was like this every night of the week down here. Not just the weekends. In the 80's, during *La Movida*, Madrid's crazy years. Did you know I own the bar next door? We used to have wild nights in there. Now it's my ruin, a shitty spirits bar for kids. An absolute disaster. But what nights we had in these two bars, and the girls, *ay,* the girls.' He was staring past us into the distance. 'I used to have an awful lot of sex in those days.'

Anyone who lived in Madrid in the 80's goes starry eyed when they speak of *La Movida*. It was what the sixties were to London or Paris, a decade that passed the Spaniards by under the strict rule of Franco. It took a while after he had gone, but eventually a Madrid based movement of young artists brought drugs, sex and endless week-long partying crashing into the Madrileños lives, another backlash against the years of oppression. What a fantastic time it must have been.

Back out in the cold we started down the street towards the Cafe Paris, a trendier place lit by red neon lights where we would play pool and drink Cacique rum and cokes served by a giant Russian named Dimitri. But tonight it was shut.

'What shall we do?' I said.

'What about the Cafe Belen, I haven't been there since your exhibition,' said Stephen.

'No way,' said Al. 'I'm not going back in there. I can't face seeing that Pablo again.'

'Why not, come on, Pablo never used to be there at this time of night, it'll be funny.' I said. Really, in more sober moments, I had no inclination to go back into the Cafe Belen either. It felt wrong to revisit the scene of our last photographic success, somehow slightly embarrassing. But with the Cacique bar shut and no other decent alternative, perhaps it wouldn't be so bad after all.

'Well, alright then,' said Al, and off we went.

Inside it was just as it always had been, candle lit tables, cool London chill out music, someone's art on the walls.

'Look at that, not a patch on our pictures,' I said.

We sat down at a round table near the window and ordered more beer. Al and I reminisced about our great night so long ago and we felt quite relaxed about being there after all.

'Oh shit!' said Al suddenly, between clenched teeth. 'I don't believe it... He's here.'

I turned round to see Pablo walking through the door. He saw us straight away, smiled, and came over.

'Ah, the great photographers, it's been a while.'

'Hello Pablo.'

'Well how are you? Still taking pictures?'

'Oh yes,' we said.

'Good. So when are you going to do another exhibition for the Belen?'

'In here?' said Al. 'Well, of course, obviously, that would be great... some time.'

'Excellent, because a space has just come up in April.'

'Ah...'

So, less than two months later and after frantic preparations, Al and I, as the only remaining members of the Extranjeros Out of Focus, had another exhibition. It took some pretty creative searching through our recent work to come up with something, but eventually we picked out eight photos each, loosely based around a profoundly conceptual theme: colour.

One way or another, by the morning of the private view, Pablo still hadn't seen a single one of our new photographs. He had trusted us to have them ready on time, but it was obvious when we turned up to hang the pictures that he was somewhat apprehensive. We weren't worried. We had, admittedly, left the framing until the last minute, but in the end we thought our bright abstract portraits and landscapes looked fantastic. Pablo examined them slowly as we placed each one on the table before him.

'Hmm. *Si*....... hmm...... *bueno. Bueno.* What is it of, this one? ... Hmm.' And so he went on, no overtures of delight. This time the expert, this quiet, withdrawn man of the arts, didn't seem to be convinced.

'Do you think he's happy?' whispered Al in my ear. I shrugged my shoulders. Things got worse when we came to hang them on the walls. Where before he had spent hours placing each work in perfect relation to the others, this time he gave up in five minutes, unable to place two colours together in any gratifying combination.

'Ba!' he said, slumping against the bar and throwing his arms wide, 'put them wherever you want.'

'I really don't think he's happy you know,' whispered Al, as we ran around trying to get them all up as quickly as possible, the sooner to be able to leave.

The party was as good as ever. We arrived late and a little drunk, relieved to find that we had missed Pablo. He had given up waiting for us and left five minutes before. Marina pressed through the crowded bar to greet us and pulled me towards a group in one corner.

'Someone from the Radio wants to meet you, she wants to do an interview!' she shouted in my ear.

'What? No, I can't cope with that now...' I thought about making a dash for the door.

'This is Ben,' said Marina, introducing me to an elegant girl in leather trousers and a black shirt.

'Right, I work for *Radio Bellas Artes* and we want to come in one day this week and interview you and the other artist live on air for our 'New Openings' feature. Which day suits you best?'

'Right.' - *Bloody hell* - 'Ah... well, um, I'd have to speak to Al of course and get back to you on that,' I said.

'Great, no problem, here's my mobile number, I expect to hear from you tomorrow, O.K.? Cool, see you soon,' and she was gone, in a cloud of cigarette smoke.

'You're joking,' said Al, who felt pretty much like me. It was all very well putting up your pictures and organising a bit of a party and wallowing in temporary, self-indulgent glory for an evening, but this was going much too far. The exhibitions kept the photography going, especially an unexpected one like this. They were the antidote to English teaching and an old excuse for weekends away, for wandering around Spain.

But going on the radio to talk about it with a super media-woman like that was just ridiculous. That belonged to a different photographic realm, the London kind, where you fight and strive and compete and talk on the radio and ruin yourself with it all. I phoned the girl the following morning, with the excuse that Al and I both worked at different times each day, and would rather not do the interview if we couldn't show up together. Still, a request for an interview was not to be dismissed entirely. We took it as a small sign of our success and told absolutely everyone. In our own minds we were heroic photographers again. The only person we hadn't managed to convince seemed to be Pablo.

A week later we decided to face him, and headed down to the Cafe Belen.

'I missed you on the opening night,' he said, 'what happened?'

'Sorry,' I said, 'we didn't mean to arrive so late.'

'Never mind. Now, this exhibition, it's... fantastic! Everyone tells me how good the place looks at the moment, thank you both, well done!'

It's nothing Pablo, really, nothing at all.

By the end of the month spring had come north to Madrid. Marina and I started to spend sunny weekends in Colmi, the little country house. What glorious days! Like a good English summer, with all its light fragrant breezes and gardening sounds. We dug out a plot for vegetables in one corner of the garden, planting token quantities of peas, leeks, tomatoes and beans in neat, ordered rows. Marina was so adept at making things grow, and so delighted when they did, that it was hard to believe she was the product of the hectic city that lay sprawling across the planes below. Back in Lavapies the *terraza* tables and chairs spilled out onto the streets from the bars, and our balcony doors spent as much time open as closed.

And then it was June, and to everyone's surprise high summer arrived with a bang: *de golpe.*

28th July 2001

¡Ayyy - Que Calor!
The heat this month really has been extraordinary. During the day it will hover between thirty-seven and forty-four degrees, and even in the dead of the coolest night it will rarely fall below twenty-four degrees centigrade. At midnight it is common to still see thirty. In the evenings Marina and I wander down to the tables on Calle Argumosa and I lean back in my chair, swamped with warmth and self-satisfaction. What a good idea it was, I think to myself, to come and live in Madrid!

By day it's insufferable. I cross the road for shade, and work in near darkness at home, the shutters bolted tight against the sun's rays. At least there is no humidity. Madrid's heat is bone dry. It's strange, then, that when the sun does fall across your bare skin, it feels so much like a very hot bath, like someone is ladling jug after jug of scalding water onto you. I long just to reach out and turn on the cold tap, or simply get out of the bath.

The only respite has been our journey to Asturias, earlier this month.

The Residents Meet Again

Early July is the last good chance to get away in Spain. After that, from the middle of the month onwards, the nation's holidays start, and the hordes hit the coasts for a month at a time, right up to mid September, when things calm down again. Marina and I headed north across the arid Burgos plains, past fields of stunted wheat and wilting trees, then over the forested Cantabrian peaks, and finally down to the coast of Asturias. To cool down, to add a little cold water. We spent a lot of time on Andrin beach. Cut away from the world, the small bay was backed by towering moss-green slopes, broken only at one end by a crumpled burgundy cliff face. In front, beyond the reach of the headlands, sat a tall, solitary island, marooned in a clear blue sea.

The water at the shore was cold. Small waves trapped the sunlight, clasped it in their closing hands, and shattered it on the soft beige undercoat of sand. Goats would occasionally appear and slowly circumvent the back of the beach, climbing every now and again to munch on ferns. The stuff of our imaginations. I thought more and more about what I knew was coming next, but decided not to say anything yet. It wasn't quite the time, and certainly not the place.

We were staying in a small hotel in a tiny hamlet near the sea, a converted mansion built long ago by a man who had made his money in South America, when Spain still had a firm colonial grip on that part of the world. A lane led away from the hotel and down to the cliffs, passing through a rolling, rich green landscape dotted with daisies, dandelions and black and white cows. We would walk down here in the evenings, stepping aside for horse-drawn carts piled high with freshly cut grass, and stopping to admire plots of enormous cabbages and runner beans.

At the end of the path, just before the low, sharp limestone cliffs fell away to the sea, was a blow hole. The ground had collapsed around it so that all we saw was a wide, grassy depression, about three metres across and two deep, at the bottom of which a tight rocky crevice emitted the most extraordinary sound. Blow holes form when the sea finds a channel through the soft limestone rock and forces its way up to the cliff top, usually bursting out in regular spouts of water. This one, however, simply issued a powerful, ghostly exhale each time an unbroken wave buffeted the cliffs below. It was like the sound of a hundred-mile-an-hour wind rushing through a tunnel deep underground. Close to, it was unnerving, but heard from a distance, sitting above the sea and staring along the coast, it was unreal.

'This place is magical,' said Marina, one evening. 'I'd love to run a small hostel in a place like this, with an Asturian veggie patch in the garden. But where would we do it? Here, or along the coast in Galicia maybe?'

'Or in the Pyrenees. Or La Rioja. No, near the sea. In San Sebastian perhaps...'

'It's impossible,' she said 'too many places to choose from.'

'Imagine if you could combine them all...'

If I could combine them all I would have no trouble coming up with a sort of composite Paradise, the perfect combination of Spanish landscapes in which to wile away eternity, or a life-time at least. I would have Andrin beach, the Basque coast and Galicia's fjords, backed by fecund Andalucian hillsides, full of fig, orange and olive trees and wild flowers. Somewhere amongst these hills the road to Andujar would appear, changing eventually into the Carrera del Darro, the cobbled lane beside the stream in Granada, which in turn would lead into the Alhambra Palace gardens, whose trickling channels of water, fruit trees and tall, manicured firs, would take me home, to the petrified forest of smooth marble pillars in Cordoba's mosque...

'You're a dreamer Ben,' said Marina, 'but it sounds wonderful, can I come with you?'

'Maybe...'

≈

When we arrived back in Madrid it felt as if we had been gone for a month. It wasn't just the shock of the intense heat again after the cool north, something new was afoot beneath the canopy of leaves below the flat. A great number of Bengalis had appeared in the street, pacing up and down in small groups, examining posters that were plastered to every available bit of wall, shop front, lamp post and tree trunk. In each there appeared a photo of a well dressed young man, and below the picture, an explanation in an indecipherable alphabet.

The smelly old bar downstairs had changed beyond recognition. It was now run by Bengalis as well. Where before we were under permanent attack from fried-fish fumes, it was now delicate oriental aromas, cumin and ginger, that drifted up through the interior *patio*. The bar itself had been emptied of its old Spanish clientele and now served jugs of water and samosas to the men who looked at the posters.

Since then, I've been writing this, heading up to Colmi every now and again for a swim, and going into the marketing company four mornings a week, where I do even less than ever. The last thing on anyone's mind as the holidays approach is learning English. Thank God for my peaceful, constructive afternoons up here in the trees.

Last Thursday, the last of the month, with my escape from the heat so near at hand, the dreaded residents meeting that I recently found advertised downstairs finally took place. Marina threw me into a flat spin by announcing that she was too busy with work and wouldn't be able to come. I tried the old 'no point in me going, won't understand a thing' routine but she quickly flattened this with the 'don't you care about your flat?' tack. She was right, the building's future was up for discussion and I had to know what was going on.

The meeting was to be held in a new venue, not far away on the Calle del Oso. I walked up the hill at seven o'clock and took the first left into a street that was bustling with shoppers. There was an old *Meson* bar and a fish shop whose windows were filled to eye level with fresh ice piled high with hake, prawns and giant, wiry crabs. The choreographed manner in which everyone appeared from the side streets and hurried in and out of shop doors, along with the leaning antiquity of the buildings and the warm evening light, reminded me of a film set. I expected to round the corner and find a camera crew lurking, hissing at me to hurry on out of shot.

But instead, as I turned into Calle Meson de Paredes I was met by the hubble-bubble of a street scene more multi-cultural than anyone could have imagined three years before. Two tall, jet-black African women, wearing colourful robes and balancing large bundles on their heads, picked their way through the dirt. (The street, like most, had been churned up for resurfacing work.) Next I passed a gaggle of portly, dark-skinned men bickering noisily outside a shop filled with big copper pots, a scene straight from an Egyptian souk. Walking on down past the old ruined church, where an impromptu brass band was performing to whoever cared to stop, I stepped aside to let three short

Andean ladies pass, their neat round faces squashed beneath billowing, blanket-wrapped loads that they carried on their backs.

Then there was a Turkish kebab shop, and along came some lanky, tongue-clicking Moroccan youths. I could be anywhere, I thought, until I glanced up at the buildings, at the wrought iron balconies, the terracotta pots and rickety shutters that could only ever be in the middle of old Madrid.

I turned into the Calle del Oso, nervous, still annoyed with Marina. I felt she almost wanted me to prove something to myself by having to go on my own. This street, also half dug up, was empty bar an old woman perched in the half darkness of her ground floor *salon*, whose doors opened out onto the pavement. She was quietly knitting, glancing up every now and again at the frenetic activity on Meson de Paredes. I wanted to stop and ask her about the history of the *barrio*, as she looked like she had been sitting there every afternoon for at least a hundred years.

The building I was looking for was a solid stone edifice with ancient, thick wooden doors. It might once have been a prison. The chubby woman who puts our bins out every night arrived at the same time and rang the correct bell. Someone buzzed us into a broad, crumbling hallway, and we climbed the twisted wooden stairs.

'My God,' she said, 'this place is even worse than ours.'

A sign above a doorway on the first floor said, 'Association of Help and Benefits for the Needy.'

'That sounds like us,' said the bins woman.

The door opened and a hunched up old lady ushered us into a small living room. She nodded towards another door opposite the first, then disappeared into a shabby kitchen. We went through.

I couldn't believe my eyes. This must have been the grandest meeting room in Lavapies! After the diminutive *salon* on the other side, it was like stepping through the looking glass. Rows of folding, red velvet seats led up to a small stage at one end. Here, a table draped in a burgundy cloth was set with two extravagant marble candelabras.

Long purple curtains framed the backdrop behind, tied aside to reveal a large 1940's black and white photograph of a proud, moustachioed Castillian man. From the general demeanour of the room, the other portrait of the young king below, and the Spanish flag in the corner, I imagined that the this must be General Franco, and that doddery die-hard fascists would still gather there to salute him on Tuesday afternoons.

I took a seat against the wall, a few rows back. Without Marina to hide behind, my Spanish trump card, I was feeling foreign again. Too much focus. I shrank into my seat, hoping to become invisible. To my relief I noticed that the woman with the worms in her beams wasn't present. But the bulbous-nosed man, who would have us all praying to the Virgin of Guadalupe, was sitting in the front row, quietly fidgeting with his clip board.

Sitting at the table on the stage were two of the residents, Mari Sol and Javier, and a young man in a suit that I didn't recognise. Mari Sol, a buxom, flaxen-haired lady, was the *presidenta* of our building, whose job it was to pay the odd bill, change passageway light bulbs, fix the TV aerial when it fell off the roof, that kind of thing. Javier was the bearded photographer from the flat below mine. They were up there as they had both volunteered themselves to help wade through the mire of bureaucracy that still separated us from having a nicely done up and strengthened block of flats.

Things got underway. Mari Sol introduced the young man next to her as a lawyer who was going to help us sort everything out. He was a flash, sharply dressed young man with neat, cropped hair and a serious, thin lipped mouth. He spoke at a rattling pace, rendering most of his early points incomprehensible:

'Crucially, wehavespokentothecouncil aboutthepossibilityof ??xxx?? the atxx??cc andhopeto x'??xxx!ise thesituationbythetime zzzxx?? nnnn??ability,' was a typical high-speed sentence, of which I could generally understand the completely unimportant half.

But an air of optimism seemed to accompany his arrival. Perhaps, we all thought, this is the person that can finally get something done. He outlined the various problems first, then Mari Sol and Javier took over, explaining everything again at greater length. There were still a few hitches standing in the way of the work on the building, inheritance problems relating to who owned one of the flats, and more bad news about the man in Germany, who really didn't want anything to do with the whole project. I was making furious notes for Marina to interpret later, but understood that everything was going quite well, especially since no one had started the inevitable descent into total-conversation chaos yet. Next came news of financial help from the council.

Mari Sol: The council have promised to pay half the costs of any work we do on the building, even if we do it bit by bit. We need to decide if we would be prepared to proceed like that, starting, for example, with the front facade.

Residents: No problem. Agreed.

Bins lady: Hang on, there's something I don't quite understand.

Saner residents (with audible sigh): Oh god...

Bins lady: I haven't agreed to do up the facade first, I know nothing about it.

Mari Sol: No, no, you see that was just an example.

Bins lady: And aren't the council meant to be paying some of this?

Mari Sol: Half of whatever you do, that's what we've all just agreed.

Bins lady (now agitated): I haven't agreed to do anything!

Mari Sol: No, but if you do then we can get financial help from the council.

Bins lady: The Council! Pah! *Nos estan toreando!* (they are bullfighting us! -giving us the run-around).

And so, as she launched into a tirade against the council, and everybody joined Mari Sol in attempting to explain to this woman just what was happening, we descended rapidly into high-decibel mayhem. The lawyer rolled his eyes, looked down in despair, then spotted a small bell on the desk in front of him. This he picked up and gave three sharp rings.

'Will you please all be quiet!' he said, and everyone was. Incredible. 'We still have an important matter to attend to and time is running out. You need to elect a new *presidenta*, because Mari Sol is coming to the end of her stint.'

I broke into a sweat... what if it was me? I couldn't do it, there was no way I could be beholden to the lunacies of this lot, and surely they would never want *me*, the foreigner, to do the president job... would they? I shrank further into my seat. How were they going to do this. Would there be a vote? Or would it be like school, where the person trying hardest not to be noticed always got picked by the teacher? Either way I thought I'd had it.

Luckily, on a purely rotational basis, the woman from 2B was chosen. To my immense relief I calculated that it would be another ten years until they got round to our flat, and thus to electing me. I would be long gone by then.

Then one of the ghostly old ladies raised a hand.

'Who on earth has bought the bar downstairs?'

'Good point,' said another, 'and what on earth is that dreadful smell they make?'

'Yes,' continued the first, 'it stinks of strange foreign herbs and spices.'

'This,' replied Mari Sol from the stage, 'is known as *Curri*, it's some sort of Indian food.'

'*Curri?*' someone murmured behind me, 'how utterly disgusting!'

'Don't worry,' said Mari Sol, 'they are only renting the bar, they haven't actually bought it.'

This calmed everyone down again. No more questions. Things seemed to be wrapping up, I was almost free. It had been almost entirely painless. In two minutes I would be half-way home. What had I been making such a fuss about? Then bulbous-nose raised his hand to query a list of accounts that the lawyer had given us all at the beginning.

'Why have some of these names got money due to them?'

Everyone pays a certain premium for upkeep and cleaning of the building at the start of each month, and although most people hardly ever paid it and had huge minus sums by their names, it seemed that others, myself included, were very much in the black.

'Look, look here,' he said, 'this bloke on the third floor, he's one hundred and eighty thousand pesetas in the black. How on earth's that? Why is he owed money and I'm not?'

My heart jumped. He was talking about me.

'Well, yes, O.K.,' said Javier from the stage, 'that's a very good example, let's have a look at that. The flat is owned by Benjamin here,' oh no! he actually pointed me out, 'he's the very newest member of our building.' Ah! Why didn't he just call me the 'foreign' one, and have me paraded up to the front! I could feel thirty pairs of eyes, even Franco's, burning into me as I sat bolt upright, smiling inanely. *Too much focus.*

'Benjamin,' he went on, 'bought his flat with no debts attached. All his fees were up to date. As we are dissolving the accounts for the repair work, to start again from scratch, Benjamin has effectively paid that amount too much, and is now due it back.'

Every mention of my name was excruciating. I was desperate to get out.

'Considering the state of the building Benjamin has bought himself into,' concluded Javier with a wry smile, 'I think we can call the money a nice, comforting little welcome present.'

A laugh rippled around the room. I knew exactly what they were thinking. 'Ha Ha, what an idiot, he actually bought himself a flat in our disastrous building!'

'Congratulations,' said a young, ginger haired man, 'do you like your present?'

I turned to look at them all. There was no hiding anymore. What a strange position I had fallen into! That first, unexpected trip to San Sebastian, a call from an academy in Madrid, a surprise job offer, a random substitute class followed by a lucky meeting with one of the students in a bar, all these fateful twists and turns had led to this, to being the centre of attention at a bizarre residents meeting in a grandiose room lost deep in the middle of Madrid.

'Yes, thank you,' I said, gritting my teeth and counting the seconds until the meeting was finally dissolved, when at last I could burst out into the street with a huge, lung-emptying, stress-relieving exhale of relief.

≈

And now I'm sitting here at my desk, thinking that if they ever do actually get round to doing up this building, it will be an occasion for another, unparalleled sigh of relief. In fact, I suppose that if I ever left Spain it would be the same, with a huge, breath-expelling swoosh of air, though not from relief, but release, for having coped with all the noise, the light, the fiesta, the romance and the excitement. Yet I'm convinced now that I would far sooner stay, keeping my breath held, that tightness in the lungs, and electricity in the brain.

I came here with no real plan, just a deep desire to escape London, to end up somewhere more interesting. I think I succeeded in that, but see that I must go one step further and stick with it, get stuck with it, proceed with this idea that's been nagging away at me, completely sure at last that it isn't another rash decision, like my coming to Spain in the first place perhaps. Now I know what to do.

I'll explain when I get back.

20th September 2001

It was always going to happen in Cornwall, no matter who it was with. Cornwall and Spain are alike in many ways. They are wild, distant peninsular masses, cut off in exile from the greater bodies of land to which they pertain. Whichever I'm in, I wish I were nearer the other.

We were down at the end of an empty, timeless valley, with a waterfall plunging down the ragged cliffs and into the sea. It was hot, beautifully hot for Cornwall. The sun was streaming in off the waves, fragmented into a million pieces, blinding me with its glare, which I somehow hoped would make things easier. Yet still my heart was pounding, my head spinning, chance after chance was missed at breaks in the conversation. It was all too much. It had to be now in case someone came along. Then someone did, a photographer who knew he was intruding, swung his tripod over his shoulder, and left. I couldn't do it now, I just wasn't able to. I stared harder into the sea, eyes watering, until at last, in a flash of determination, I got it out in Spanish:

'Quieres casarte conmigo?'

≈

She said yes, and so it is that Marina and I are engaged. What a horrible phrase, better 'going to get married'. I will be married not just to her, but to Spain, because I know she wouldn't want to go and live a life in England. Never mind. I'm happy to risk a life out here, and leave some latter part of my original, English one un-lived. I know we will be stuck in Madrid for a long while yet, but I still have high hopes of finally living near the coast, in deep green Asturias, or the Basque country perhaps.

The aging Spanish drunks are back in the bar downstairs again, having finally accepted the new owners and crawled back in by force of habit, noses screwed up at the strong smell of 'curri'. Madrid is vibrant, refreshed, everybody back from their holidays at last, a new cycle beginning. It is September, the city's most beautiful month, when the sun's intensity softens a little and takes on a silvery glow, drawing breath back into the streets and coaxing us from soporific summer pools, as we chart new, meandering courses through the changes in our lives.

Epilogue: One Year On

'And where did you say you wanted to get married?'

'El Escorial'

'O.K. Well, everything seems to be in ord... Oh dear.'

'What is it?'

'Benjamin, you don't seem to have any parents.'

'What?'

Marina and I were in Madrid's central records office, negotiating the first steps of the civil marriage process. The women across the table was obviously a very heavy smoker, as a rank, ashy smell drifted across the table every time she spoke in her deep, croaky voice.

'You see there are no parental names on your birth certificate. I don't know if this is any good.'

'But I've had that all my life, it's a standard English Birth certificate.'

'No it isn't, I've seen bigger ones than this with the parents' names written at the bottom. This is different.'

'Listen, there is nothing wrong with this piece of paper, it's been translated and certified by the foreign office and as far as I know my parents are my parents!'

'Alright, fine, we'll just have to see if the judge accepts it. If you don't hear from us in two weeks then there's no problem and you can get on with your plans.' Where had I heard that before? Was the entire process of organising a wedding in Spain going to be like this?

≈

Two weeks later I went up to the town council in El Escorial to drop off the next round of documents and confirm the date of the wedding. The council building was a vast granite edifice overlooking a sunlit plaza, beyond which the Monastery's tall spires rose above the town roofs. With the Catholic church ruled out on grounds of faith, we had chosen this as the perfect place for a civil ceremony.

'Hello, I want to get married here in July,' I said to a crooked-toothed security guard just inside the door.

'Hmm, I think you need the second floor for that.'

Up on the second floor I found a door that said '*Juzgado*'. I knocked and a man came out to ask what I wanted.

'Third floor,' he said.

On the third floor I found an office marked 'Registry'. Inside a woman with short blonde hair was sitting behind a desk piled high with paperwork, sneezing hard into a handkerchief.

'*Jesus*,' I said, which is Spanish for 'bless you'.

'Can I help?' she asked.

'I want to hand in my wedding documents, we're getting married here in July.'

'Ah, well in that case you probably want the floor below.'

'They sent me up here.'

'Oh. You see the thing is the woman who usually deals with all this isn't here.'

'Well I was just told to bring in these documents but I'm not really sure what to do after that.'

'Neither am I!' she said, sneezing again. 'Let's have a look anyway...'

She reached up to a bookshelf full of ragged leather-bound volumes and pulled down a folder containing various stapled documents, one of which was labelled '*Matrimonio*'.

'Ah! Lets see if this helps.' She began to flick through, a bewildered look spreading across her face, then stopped suddenly and asked 'What day did you say you were getting married?'

'The first Saturday in July.'

'Impossible.'

'What? Why?'

'We don't marry that weekend. Hang on, I'll just check the diary... No, out of the question, it's not even a stand-by weekend.'

'But we sent a fax and a letter two months ago...' I felt a familiar desperation creeping in. The honeymoon and the caterers were already booked, most of the English contingent had already bought their flights. 'Everything was fine when we rang last week.'

'Sorry, it can't have been. The judge doesn't come in that weekend.'

'But a councillor was going to come in and do it.'

'A councillor?'

'Yes, unless the Mayor could make it at the last minute.'

'Are you getting married with the council or the judge?'

'Council I suppose.' What the hell was the difference?

'Then you need the bottom floor.'

'Right. Fine. Who do I ask for?'

'I don't know, you see the woman who usually deals with all this isn't here...'

On the ground floor the security guard pointed me to a man in an information booth.

'I was hoping to get married here in July and want to know just where I'm meant to hand in these papers.'

'Are you sure?'

'Sure?'

'Sure you want to get married.'

'-?'

'We hand out a special lawyer's card with every wedding in case of divorce.'

'Oh.'

'Only joking! You need the first floor.'

On the first floor a smiling, middle-aged woman ushered me into a small office. I pled my case and files were consulted.

'Ah, yes, Benjamin Curtis, first Saturday in July, no problem, it's all fixed. All you need to do is leave your documents with Maria on the third floor.'

With a mixture of growing frustration and disbelief, I climbed back up to the third floor.

'They've sent me back,' I said to the lady with the cold, 'someone called Maria needs to see these.'

'Ah, Maria is the woman who usually deals...'

'Yes, yes, she isn't here, but can I *please* just leave all this paperwork for her?'

'O.K., I'll take it and leave her a note. What date was this for again?'

I told her.

'But we don't marry that weekend.'

Ahhhhh!!! 'I'm being done by the council, remember?'

'Oh yes, so you are! *Achewww!*'

'*Jesus!*'

The road down through the pass on the way back to Madrid was thick with swirling white seed heads from the spring flowers, floating on the air like big fluffy snow flakes. Everything will be alright, I kept telling myself, there are still two months to go.

≈

'*Wrong one.*'

'What?' Marina was speaking between clenched teeth, from behind a fixed smile.

'*Wrong. Ring.*'

I looked down and found that I was sliding my enormous ring onto her slender finger. Quickly I slid it off again, made the swap, and pushed hers carefully over her knuckle. Phew, nobody seemed to have noticed. We were up on the first floor of the council building, standing at the front of a long, stately conference room. Behind us sat a hundred and forty assorted English and Spanish guests, gently perspiring. Seven o'clock in the evening, up here in the hills, and still the heat was insufferable.

The councillor pushed a sheet of paper across the table towards us. It was a script, the wedding vows, three lines a piece, the first I'd seen of them in my life. I read out my bit, coming completely unstuck on the Spanish half-way through. There was some muffled laughter from the back. Marina spoke next, then the councillor brought things to a close, his indecipherable words drifting away above our heads.

And then we were outside the main door of the building, being pelted with rice and rose petals, laughing together. 'Kiss her, kiss her,' came shouts from the crowd. It was unreal, all part of the chaotic sequence of events that had been going on for a fortnight - the hectic days preparing Colmi for the reception, the heated arguments, arrival of friends and relatives - all culminating in this. 'I am married... married!' I repeated over and over to myself in disbelief, as Marina's brother drove us back down to the house for the party.

Colmi's garden looked magnificent, a mid-summer night's dream. The terrace above the garage was bedecked with plants and Virginia vines that crept along the railings. Hibiscus and sweet-smelling, star-flowered jasmine lined the steps up to the house, and lavender, moon daisies and roses sprang up from freshly dug borders. The pool, and the circular tables laid for supper that surrounded it, were softly lit by lights that my father had put up in the trees, and the branches' reflections rippled slowly across the water's surface as it started to get dark.

At ten o'clock everybody sat down to eat, and almost at once the playful heckling began: '*Que se besen,*' the call for the kiss from Marina's university friends on the other side of the pool, and 'Speech, speech!' from some delinquent English friends at the back. Trouble makers. I had told them all long ago that, to my immense relief, Spanish weddings involved absolutely no speeches. But they simply wouldn't give up.

Lucky then that I'd been running a few lines through my head for several months, just in case of emergency. I stood up on my chair, a glass of wine in one hand, and thanked everybody enthusiastically for coming, first in Spanish, then English. Looking down I noticed the in-laws eying me rather suspiciously, and thought it best to round things off as quickly as possible.

'*Un Brindis,*' I shouted, 'a toast, to Marina: *Viva La Novia!* Long Live The Bride!' To which everybody lifted their glasses, and the Spaniards replied in the traditional way, their happy cries filling the balmy night air:

'¡*Viva La Novia, Viva Marina, VIVA!*'

Errant in Iberia

Also by Ben Curtis:

<u>Notes from Spain</u>

News, podcasts, photography, life, comment, contact…
www.notesfromspain.com

832082

Printed in Great Britain by
Amazon.co.uk, Ltd.,
Marston Gate.